A COLLECTOR'S GUIDE TO

Autographs

WITH PRICES

BOB BENNETT

Cover Design: Ann Eastburn
Interior Layout: Anthony Jacobson

Library of Congress Catalog
Card Number 85-051707

ISBN 0-87069-460-X

Copyright © 1986
Wallace-Homestead Book Company

10 9 8 7 6 5 4 3 2 1

Published by

Wallace-Homestead Book Company
580 Waters Edge
Lombard, Illinois 60148

One of the
ABC PUBLISHING
Companies

Contents

Acknowledgments

Thanks are due to all of the autograph collectors and dealers who have assisted me with this project, including Russ Amacher, Roger Christensen, Jack Good, Jim Larson, Monroe Mendoza, Eric Niderost, Bill Rohrs, Bob Rubin, Mike Shaw, Sy Sussman, Georgia Terry, Jim Weaver, and all of the contributors to my magazines, *Newsreel* and *Autograph Digest.* I wish to thank my father, Robert W. Bennett, for photographing items from my collection, as well as Robert Minkin, Movie Star News, Sy Sussman, and T.C.M.A., Ltd. Assistance with preparing the manuscript on computer was provided by Brian Rapalje and his family. For helpful suggestions on the manuscript I wish to thank Tom Bene-Trono, Jay Fayette, Brian Rapalje, Pat Reardon, and Dick Thweatt.

Introduction

Collecting autographs — the hobby of obtaining the signatures of well-known personalities of the past and present, is one of the world's oldest and most respected hobbies. The thousands of autograph collectors in the United States and the rest of the world range from youngsters who wait eagerly at ballparks for their favorite players to sign scorecards or bubble gum cards to millionaire investors such as publisher Malcolm Forbes, who has accumulated a very valuable and historically important collection of signed letters and documents. Like Forbes, many collectors concentrate solely on historical material, the letters and documents signed by great personages of the past such as presidents, authors, and world leaders. Other collectors prefer the autographs of modern authors, astronauts, movie stars, cartoonists, or sports figures. Signed photographs of personalities are very popular with many collectors, but autographed letters, or just plain signatures on scraps of paper or index

Jackie Robinson signed 1950 baseball card, **$40.**

cards, are also widely sought. Autograph collecting means different things to different people, and there seems to be enough room in the field to encompass a wide variety of tastes and interests.

Movie scene signed by Dan Aykroyd, **$15**

Autograph collecting began about two thousand years ago in ancient Rome. The Roman statesman Cicero, probably the first collector, assembled a collection of letters signed by the most important people of his time, which included one from Julius Caesar. No one can find Caesar's letter today, but, if it could be located, it would be worth over two million dollars. It wasn't until the nineteenth century, however, that autograph collecting became widespread. Queen Victoria of Great Britain began collecting autographs as a young girl, and her collection is now important enough to be displayed at Windsor Castle, the home of Queen Elizabeth II. In the United States, several individuals started autograph collections early in our history, which helped to preserve the letters and documents signed by the American Founding Fathers. Later collectors wrote to famous personalities to request their autographs through the mail and began to seek out and pay Congressional pages to acquire the autographs of the nation's political leaders. In the last half of this century, autograph dealers came into existence as the increasing numbers of collectors found it difficult to obtain material signed by deceased personalities. One autograph dealership, Walter R. Benjamin Autographs, Inc., is still in operation and is now under the direction of Benjamin's daughter, Mary. It remains one of the most successful and reputable businesses in the field.

It wasn't until 1948 that the first organization for autograph collectors, The Manuscript Society, was formed for collectors of historical letters and documents. A more popular autograph society, the Universal Autograph Collectors Club, was organized in the New York area in 1965 under the leadership of Harold W. Rapp, Jr. The Manuscript Society and the Universal Autograph Collectors are still in existence and have been joined by many other small organizations and independent publications that are discussed at the end of this book.

Autograph collecting has steadily increased in stature and popularity through the years. One collector who contributed significantly to the growth of the hobby is author Charles Hamilton. He established an auction house devoted solely to autographs in the 1960s and wrote several important books about the subject, such as *Scribblers and Scoundrels* (1968) and *The Signature of America* (1979). The first person to denounce the Hitler diaries as forgeries, Hamilton is also responsible for introducing the word "philography," meaning the study or collecting of autographs.

GERALD R. FORD

August 6, 1979

Dear Mr. and Mrs. Miglis:

Mrs. Ford and I were delighted to learn that you
will be celebrating the joyous occasion of your
60th Wedding Anniversary on August 10. We join
with your family and friends in extending warm
congratulations and best wishes.

The fact that you can celebrate such a distinctive
anniversary is an eloquent tribute to the quality
of caring and sharing which you brought to your
marriage.

May this happy day usher in another year of good
health and much enjoyment.

Warmest best wishes,

Jerry Ford

Mr. and Mrs. Frank Miglis
c/o Bob Bennett
1 Governor's Lane
Shelburne, Vermont 05482

Letter signed by Gerald Ford, **$75.**

Autograph collecting has a history filled with stories of forgers and fakers that makes the philographer's task more challenging, interesting, and sometimes more worthwhile. There are many dangers that the autograph collector must learn to recognize before buying and investing in autographs. Avoiding disreputable dealers and forgers and signatures that are not genuine — signatures signed by machines, rubber stamps, or secretaries — are a few pitfalls we will present ways to overcome in this book. But for the present, the question might be asked: "Why do people collect autographs with all the problems and dangers inherent to them?"

There are several answers to this question.

One of the major reasons people collect autographs is because of the tremendous historical value they possess. Both major and minor historians have been known to bungle historical facts, sometimes because they lacked the documents that might prove their theses. Autographs can document history and often provide insight into the signer's personality, even possible mental disorders, or the person's views of his or her times. Autograph collecting can also make the collector more knowledgeable about history and the lives of famous people of the past or present. There are few better methods

Dear Bob,

I recived your letter requesting my autograph and I am very flattered. I too collect autographs of "famous people", but I don't consider myself one! Some of the autographs that I have collected over to years include such great people as: Ginger Rogers, Fred Astaire and Groucho Marx(my hero). So you can see why I don't consider myself in the same class as these people.

To help you alomg with your collection, I am enclosing Elton John's adress, but please, along with mine, keep discreet.

Once again, thank you for wanting to add mine to your collection. Good Luck.

Gratefully Yours,

Alice Cooper

Typed letter discussing autograph collecting signed by singer Alice Cooper, **$12.**

of self-education than reading quotations and statements from famous people that are often contained in autographed documents. In addition, collectors who write to celebrities through the mail must often research the life of the person whose autograph they desire in order to compose an informed letter that will be most likely to elicit the best response.

Autographs are also collected because they have a personal meaning to the collector. If a great or famous personality signs an autograph for you, they are taking time from their important lives to do something for you, and, in effect, the autograph has created a bond between you and the famous personality. Although autograph collecting can be a form of hero worship, it is usually only a recognition of achievement on the part of the collector. Autograph collectors are not just blind followers of the famous. Collectors are often successful in their own right, many being doctors, lawyers, or even authors. Many famous people have been or are collectors. President John F. Kennedy, Senator Mark Hatfield, actors Glenn Ford and Carol Burnett, and singer Alice Cooper, are several who come to mind. Sometimes, collectors give autographed photographs and letters from their collections to friends or relatives for birthdays or other special occasions. When these gifts are prepared in advance and contain personal inscriptions from the recipient's favorite personalities, they make wonderful and appreciated mementoes that are treasured for many years.

Finally, autographs are collected because they have great monetary value. Historical documents from history's great names can be worth thousands of dollars, depending on the person and the type of autograph in question (letter, photograph, etc.). Signatures of living personalities can also command high prices, especially if the autographs are on interesting or worthwhile items or on letters with especially good content. Even mere signatures can be worth a great deal. Every time Ronald Reagan signs a piece of paper, it is immediately worth at least $50. The reclusive actress Greta Garbo could receive at least $500 for each signature from her pen. Good content letters written by people as diverse as Neil Armstrong, Richard Nixon, James Cagney, or Salvador Dali — which you might be able to obtain through the mail — could be worth upwards of $100 apiece. Autographs are one of the most profitable investments of all collectibles.

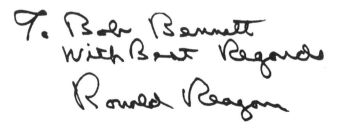

Signature of Ronald Reagan inscribed to the author, **$60**.

Greta Garbo

Greta Garbo autograph, **$500.**

Collecting autographs can open many doors for you. It can lead you into the world of rare and valuable historical documents or bring you in contact with your favorite celebrities in a variety of fields. There are pitfalls to avoid, but many joys to be experienced. Welcome to this truly wonderful hobby!

1

Autographs As Investments

Autographs are among the rarest of all collectibles, and some can be the most valuable. In a given year, for example, only about fifty autographs of George Washington appear on the market, and at substantial prices, depending on the importance of the item. Because more than 90 percent of all Washington autographs (and of most other famous historical names) belong to private or public institutions, few are likely to be offered for sale at any time in the future. The increased demand for many autographs in recent years, coupled with the great rarity of many autographs, make autograph collecting a hobby that can yield high profits to the knowledgeable investor. Yet, there are dangers that must be avoided if you are to make money with autographs. In this chapter, we will examine the autograph as an investment and look into the reason for an autograph's value. We shall also discuss the types of autographs that make the best investments.

As with any other commodity, the prices of autographs are determined by supply and demand. Supply refers to the rarity or scarcity of the item and its effect upon price. Demand measures the intensity of people's preference for the item. In autographs, demand is usually more important than scarcity, since the rarest autographs are often those of people whose autographs were never widely sought after or who have been forgotten, with the result that their autographs have not been saved. The autographs of minor politicians or minor sports players, such as a baseball player who appeared in only one game in 1926 and failed to get a hit, are probably much more difficult to find than autographs of Richard Nixon or Steve Garvey. But, since virtually no one wants the signatures of unknown personalities, a Nixon or Garvey autograph would command a higher price. In a few instances, rarity alone can cause an autograph to be highly priced. One example is the signature of

Handwritten letter signed by George Washington, **$3,500.**

a signer of the Declaration of Independence, Button Gwinnett. Gwinnett was hardly the most noteworthy of the signers, yet his signature is worth the most because of the scarcity of examples. Most of his letters and signatures were burned in the late eighteenth century. In 1979, a document signed by Gwinnett in 1773 sold for $100,000. Gwinnett's signature is important for completing a collection of signers of the Declaration of Independence, so it is not a signature that is lacking some sort of demand.

Besides supply and demand, the condition of the item and its content or importance also help to determine value. If a signature is smeared, dirty, faded, torn, or damaged in some other manner, the item becomes less desirable and lower in price. Condition of

an item, in virtually all cases, will shape the price of the signature, but a damaged item could still have tremendous value. A letter handwritten by Abraham Lincoln during the Civil War to a dying soldier's wife, for example, would command a very high price no matter what the condition of the piece. Condition would not be the major factor in determining price in this instance. Another Lincoln letter, the famous note sent to the young girl, Grace Bedell, who suggested that Lincoln grow a beard, was sold to television producer David L. Wolper ("Roots") for $20,000, despite the fact that it was water stained. Apparently, Grace had opened the letter while walking home from the post office on a snowy day.

If the item is less important, its condition is much more pertinent. A simple signature of Ronald Reagan's is worth about $50 to $75, but if torn, water stained, or severely smudged, the price might fall below $20. Aside from the condition or importance of the item (historically important letters or documents are usually worth the most), the form of the autograph will also influence the value. Most collectors prefer letters that are completely handwritten by the personality. These are worth the most. Simple signatures on index cards or slips of paper are generally worth the least. In the case of letters, the content is most important. A letter from President Franklin D. Roosevelt that discusses his economic philosophy and the New Deal is worth far more than a letter of his ordering stationery supplies.

In regard to the value of autographs, an important point must be kept in mind. Autographs, like all other commodities, have no inherent value. In other words, they have no worth apart from the value that consumers place upon them. Changing consumer preferences give an autograph its value. An autograph of Michael Jackson on one of his record albums is currently worth about $100. But in five years, if Jackson is forgotten and his popularity declines, the same signed album may only be worth $10. In twenty more years, should Jackson become a musical legend, the album's value might surge to $200. Value is based entirely on consumer preferences. Some autograph collectors make unwise investments in autographs because they fail to note this fact. Other collectors believe that certain autographs are more valuable than they actually are because they see value as something other than consumer valuations. For

example, some collectors of movie star autographs sell the autographs of American movie stars for less money because it costs more in postage to obtain the autographs of foreign stars. Although there is a grain of truth in this argument (since postage costs are greater, collectors are less likely to send for foreign stars' autographs and hence they will be more scarce), the argument is fallacious. If consumers place a higher value on the autograph of Raquel Welch, than they do on Brigitte Bardot, then all other things being equal (supply, condition, etc.), the autograph of Welch will be more valuable. It doesn't matter how much money you put into obtaining an autograph; if consumers do not place a high value upon it, it will not be very valuable.

Although we have been referring to autographs as "investments" in this chapter, autographs and other collectibles are not exactly investments if we use that term correctly. An investment is the allocation of savings in a way that will make future production and the creation of new goods or services possible. Autographs and other collectibles are desirable in and of themselves, but produce nothing. The only possible way to actually invest in autographs is to purchase a firm that works to find autographs or that writes to famous personalities to obtain autographs.

The fact that autographs and other collectibles are not exactly investments helps to show us some of the dangers inherent in "investing" in autographs. Over three hundred years ago in Holland, an important lesson for collectors of almost anything can be found. Rare tulips were imported to Holland from the Near East and soon became widely collected. Horticultur- ists began to hybridize and crossbreed the flowers, creating new and exotic variations that became very valuable. Prices skyrocketed, speculators entered the field, and a frenzy known as the "Tulip Mania" followed when speculators tried to find a bigger fool than themselves to purchase the bulbs at a higher price than they had paid. Eventually, the high prices could not be sustained and the bubble burst. Many lost huge sums of money. The lesson here is simple: Since collect- ibles do not produce new wealth, they can be dangerous risks when they are purchased in a wildly inflated market. If values are artificially raised by the activities of speculators, eventually the market will self-correct and prices will drop accordingly.

The most dangerous collectibles, in my view, are those falling in the fad category. Autographs, since they are oftentimes historically or culturally important, are much safer collectible acquisitions. Collectibles such as beer cans, belt buckles, or baseball cards may not be as risk free.

Related to a speculative frenzy is the problem of currency debasement, or inflation, caused by an increase in the supply of money. Inflation makes our dollars worth less and "bids up" the prices of commodities. During the 1970s, a decade of high inflation, the prices of most collectibles soared. In 1971, for example, the signature of the famed movie star Lon Chaney was selling for about $20. By 1977 the price had risen to $75, and by 1979 it had mushroomed to $550. Today Lon Chaney's autograph is worth close to $1,000. Although we have recently observed a decline in the inflation rate (or more exactly, a decline in the Consumer Price Index) without the

onset of a major recession or depres- sion, periods of high inflation are usually followed by a recessionary period. During a recession, people tend to buy less, and purchases are usually limited to vital necessities. When people have less money to spend on frivolities such as collect- ibles, prices usually plummet. After all, if you are trying to feed your family, a signed photograph of Marilyn Monroe won't be of much help to you. It might be argued that there will always be some rich people who will buy your collectibles, but the number of rich people with money to spend on col- lectibles will surely decline, and in a recession this will lower prices. It is unlikely we will have a recession severe enough to destroy the value of the best autographs and documents, but that a recession will substantially lessen the value of many of the less

Because of the extreme scarcity of authentic examples, signed photographs of vintage movie stars continue to increase in value. Harold Lockwood, **$100.**

Olive Thomas, **$175.**

important autographs is certainly not out of the question. You can probably take heart in the fact that since recessions are usually followed by renewed inflation, quality purchases made during the down time may turn out to be excellent investments at a later date.

Keeping the dangers of inflation and speculative frenzies in mind, there are several ways to improve your chances of making money with autographs and avoiding possible losses. The first thing to remember is that you should seek out quality above all else. This

15

Virginia Pearson, **$50.**

means that you should look for material having either historical or cultural value or that which is interesting and unique. Although the autographs of Washington, Napoleon, Jefferson, and Lincoln are always excellent choices, autographs of great authors or musicians of the past are also worthwhile. Further, it is not necessary to concentrate on individuals of the past. Autographs of living sports stars, great film stars, or even rock musicians, if carefully selected, should also make good investments. The test of a good investment is whether you think the person is a good bet to be remembered in the future. Learn to spot the capricious areas and individuals whom you believe will be popular for only a short time period. Some current fads in the autograph hobby are collecting the autographs of *Playboy* playmates or stamp designers. In my view, these are not good bets for the future.

Mae Murray, **$50.**

Aside from collecting famous personalities, try to collect items that are interesting and unique. I have encountered an early woodcut of the moon signed by Neil Armstrong; Christian Barnaard's recollections of his first heart transplant; Roger Maris's thoughts before, during, and after hitting his record-setting sixty-first home run; and a letter from Marilyn Monroe describing her favorite film roles and listing her favorite films. To build an important and valuable collection, you must really use your imagination to think of some exciting, one-of-a-kind items that you can purchase or obtain through the mail.

Bessie Love, **$30.**

It is quite possible to tailor your collection to your area(s) of interest and expertise. If history is your favorite subject, you should pursue the autographs of historical figures. If your field of interest is baseball or the movies or literature, then you are better off collecting in those categories. You will be more comfortable in choosing the personalities who are the most highly regarded and worthy of collecting in fields you already enjoy. It is also a good idea to specialize. If you stretch out too much, it is unlikely that your varied collections will be impressive. Try to be definitive within one or two fields.

Scene from *Tarzan* signed by "Jane" Maureen O'Sullivan, **$15.**

It is also important to be able to detect forgeries and other unauthentic autographs, to have a good knowledge of autograph prices, and to know how to find the right dealers in your area of specialty. Then you must learn how to preserve autographs yourself or find someone else who does this work. As we have already suggested, know what determines the price of an autograph and be aware of the dangers in investing in collectibles. This book will be able to help you with all of the aforementioned, but to become an expert, you will need to do additional reading and research. (A list of helpful books and publications is included at the end of the book.) It is not absolutely necessary to become an expert in autographs to enjoy the hobby.

However, if you approach the hobby from a financial, speculative standpoint, becoming an expert is a good idea.

Some other tips for making sound investments in autographs are the following: buy or obtain autographs that are most easily liquidated, i.e., those easy to sell to others; buy items with a high unit value. (If you need to sell quickly, it is best to have only a few items to sell rather than hundreds of items.) Buy during or after a recessionary situation, not before it.

Since autographs can withstand the test of time and often have tremendous historical and cultural value (think of how important such items as Thomas Jefferson's first draft of the Declaration of Independence or Edgar

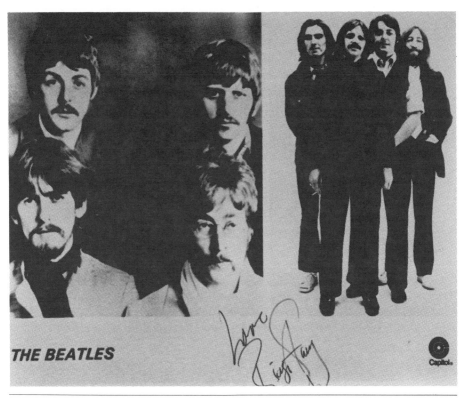

Photograph of the Beatles signed by Ringo Starr, **$40.**

Signed sketch of Woody Woodpecker by Walter Lantz (© Walter Lantz Productions), **$15.**

Allan Poe's original manuscript for *The Pit and the Pendulum* are), they can provide very profitable returns for careful collectors. If you are aware of the dangers of investing in autographs, and remember to avoid fads and search out quality, you, too, can put together a first rate collection of autographs that will increase in value in the future.

2

Buying Autographs

Once you begin collecting autographs, you will find that many you want to add to your collection are hard to locate. You may have trouble finding individuals who sell autographs, or, if you write to various personalities to obtain their signatures through the mail (see Chapter 3), you will, of course, limit yourself to autographs of living people. Autographs just can't be found where you find other collectibles. You won't stumble upon an authentic Thomas Jefferson letter at a flea market or used bookstore. Occasionally, want ads in the local paper may help you to find smaller sources for a few autographs, but to make educated decisions regarding the purchase of these autographs, you must acquire a knowledge of prices and the authentication of autographs. To acquire the desirable, genuine autographs that you cannot find for yourself, you must resort to buying at auctions conducted by reputable dealers or firms or through the catalogs of respected autograph dealers. In this chapter, we will direct you to these

sources, offer tips on buying autographs, and help you to gain a working knowledge of prices and an understanding of the terminology used in a dealer's catalog.

Many of the more experienced collectors find that they can acquire the best material at the lowest possible prices through auctions. There are several autograph auction houses, including the Scriptorium in Beverly Hills and Kelleher's in Massachusetts, and a number of other auctions that are conducted only by mail. If you have a thorough knowledge of prices, auctions may be your best source. Some auctions make it easier for the less experienced collector by setting minimum bids or price guidelines on the items for sale. Since some of the best material, i.e., historically important documents, is available by auction, auctions are certainly something you should pursue. One of the best auctions for the beginner is the annual auction of the Universal Autograph Collectors Club (UACC), usually held in late June in New York City

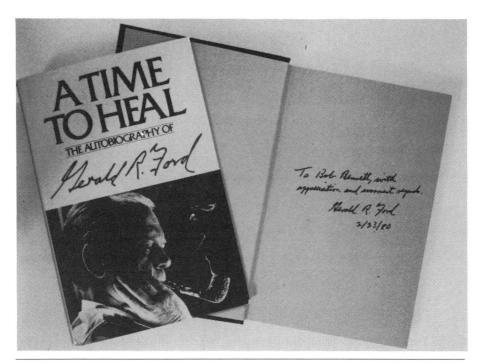

Dealers often sell items that are difficult for most collectors to obtain through the mail. Signed presidential memoirs, Gerald Ford, **$75.**

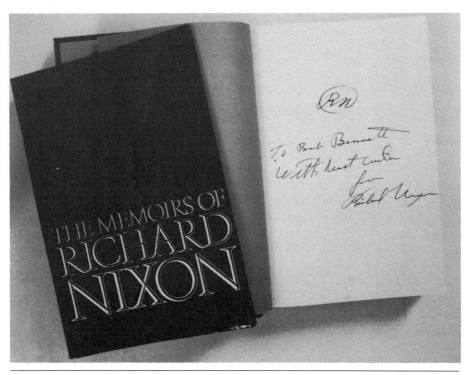

Richard Nixon presidential memoirs, **$75.**

Signed photograph of the legendary Fred Astaire and Ginger Rogers dancing team sold by a dealer for **$25.**

(auction catalogs are mailed to all members in May). There is no need to attend the auction, as you may also bid by mail. The UACC auctions offer a wealth of material in virtually all fields and prices, from very important historical items to movie stars' or sports players' signatures on file cards. In addition, the UACC also holds conventions in many major cities where you can meet other collectors and dealers and purchase autographs. These conventions are an excellent experience for all collectors and can help you make contact with dealers who sell autographs in your area of interest. The UACC also helps you find autograph dealers through listing you as a new member in its club publication, *The Pen and Quill.* The many dealers who read *The Pen and Quill* will add your name to their mailing list and send you catalogs. If you do not purchase from these dealers after three or four mailings, your name will

Dear Robert,

I regret to say that I have no photographs to send out. I usually let the studio send out stills for the latest film. But I want you to know I appreciate your letter and kind words! Best wishes

Meryl Streep

Handwritten note (A.N.S.) signed by actress Meryl Streep, **$10.**

probably be removed from their list. A polite letter sent to the dealer may prevent this from happening. Most dealers like to keep a large mailing list of possible customers and will honor requests for catalog mailings.

Auctions are important sources, but, if you wish to obtain the highest quality historical material, most of your autograph purchases will probably be from autograph dealers. Every dealer should at least be a member of the UACC, which has an Ethics Board to help settle any dispute between collectors and dealers. Membership in the club does not automatically guarantee that the dealer is honest. Some dealers, inexperienced in certain areas, could make mistakes regarding the authenticity of some items. Others have been known to sell autographs signed by machines, secretaries, rubber stamps, or even forged autographs.

Yet, there are enough experts in the club so that disreputable and inexperienced dealers have failed to survive in the business. For historical autograph dealers, membership in the Manuscript Society, an organization devoted to collecting documents and manuscripts, is also a minimum requirement. Reputable autograph dealers have "money-back guarantees of authenticity" stating that the dealer will refund your money if the autograph is found not to be authentic, no matter how many years have passed since it was purchased. It is the responsibility of the dealer, not the collector, to make sure that autographs are genuine. The guarantee is usually separate from a "return privilege" given by a dealer, which allows you to return an autograph within a certain period of time if the autograph is not to your satisfaction.

Dear Friend:

I hope you will pardon this little burst of enthusiasm but I have just seen Paul Fejos' remarkable picturization of LONESOME, in its final form - that is, in the form in which it will eventually reach you - and I want very much to share with you the tenderness, the loveliness, the sympathy and joy of this very unusual picture.

When first I saw it, it had not yet been synchronized with sound effects, music and dialogue. But even then I knew that Paul Fejos had wrought a masterpiece of direction out of Mann Page's lovely story.

And now - after seeing and HEARING it for the first time I hope you will indulge me just this once and let me give full vent to my enthusiasm. It seems to me that LONESOME is the perfect combination of sound, music and dialogue . . . or as my son Junior expressed it . . . "talk where talking is appropriate and silence where silence is golden".

Some of my friends and associates who sat in the projection room with me said that they had never seen anything like it before . . others expressed their belief that it was the perfect picture. For myself, I am satisfied that LONESOME is different - refreshingly different - that the merging of Fejos' masterful direction and the imaginative writing of the author comes very close to genius.

I am also satisfied that when you hear the delicious dialogue between these two lonely youngsters - who are the only main characters in the drama - Glenn Tryon as the punch presser and Barbara Kent as the telephone operator, you will feel the same tenderness towards them that I felt - the same yearning desire to see them find each other after they have been parted by the crowds -- the same wholesome satisfaction with the ending.

And now, with all my heart, I hope that you will see LONESOME because I know you'll enjoy it -- whether you see the silent version or see and hear the version with sound effects.

Sincerely yours,

Carl Laemmle

CARL LAEMMLE

November 12th, 1928.

An important T.L.S. signed by early film mogul Carl Laemmle, **$65.**

For example, if you were dissatisfied with the condition of the item. When you receive a catalog from a dealer, carefully read the terms of sale to discover if the dealer has a satisfactory guarantee, whether payment is required in advance, and what time period you have to return the items purchased.

Autograph catalogs also contain many abbreviations that you must understand to be sure of what you are buying. A few of these are listed here.

A.L.S., Autograph Letter Signed. A letter completely handwritten and signed by the person in question.

L.S., Letter Signed. The letter may be written by a secretary or typed (T.L.S.) but is actually signed by the person in question.

Ms.S., Manuscript Signed. A signed poem, story, play, or typescript.

D.S., Document Signed. An official government or legal paper, including a signed bank check or receipt.

S.P., Signed Photograph. This is usually followed by information as to the type of photograph (e.g., black and white or "matt finished") and the size, given either in inches or in terms used by book printers, such as folio (about 12" by 19"); quarto (about 9½" by 12"); octavo (about 6" by 8"); duodecimo (about 5" by 7⅜"); or crown sixteenmo (about 3¾" by 5").

In addition, there are other terms relating to signatures and documents that are useful for you to know. The term "frank" refers to a signature on an envelope by a president or member of Congress that permits the letter to be delivered free of charge. The term "foxed" relates to condition and means that the letter or document has yellowish brown stains, usually caused by water damage. If an item is described as "vintage", it means that it was signed during a person's prime rather than old age and might indicate that the signature is more firm and attractive. "Inscribed" means that the item was signed to a specific person, such as "To Joe."

When you receive a dealer's catalog through the mail, be aware that many other collectors will be receiving the catalog at the same time. It is important to contact the dealer as soon as possible if you are interested in any of the items. Most dealers list their telephone numbers in their catalogs, so it is wise to place your order or reserve items by telephone whenever possible. You will be asked to pay for your items in advance until your credit has been established. Although telephone orders are recommended, there are always some items offered that you may acquire by mail order. The point to remember is that you should not give up on an item if you are unable to reach the dealer by telephone, or if you receive the catalog late, or if you simply do not have the time to call the dealer.

Handwritten, signed quote (A.Q.S.) by poet Allen Ginsberg, **$15.**

Signed musical quote by Cole Porter, **$750.**

This signed photograph of burlesque star Lili St. Cyr is unusual because Ronald Reagan is in the audience (behind St. Cyr and looking up from the center table). **$20.**

The most difficult part of buying autographs is in finding reputable dealers who sell the type of material you are interested in at a reasonable price. Joining the UACC will, as we have stated, place you on many dealers' mailing lists, but it won't necessarily place you in contact with the dealers best suited to meet your needs. At the end of this book, you will find a list of the names and addresses of many dealers in different fields who are all reputable and conscientious. Also listed is a small, inexpensive pamphlet published by autograph dealer Georgia Terry, titled *The Autograph Dealers Directory* that also lists reputable dealers you will find most helpful. Once you know who some of the trusted dealers are, you will find it much easier to make a decision about whom to patronize.

Like collectors, many dealers specialize in certain areas, although there are some dealers who handle all types of material. Oftentimes the dealers who specialize are the top experts in their field, and they are able to offer the best prices and the most carefully selected material. However, the president of the UACC, Herman M. Darvick, sells autographs in many areas, and is one of the leading authorities in almost all fields of the hobby. I recommend that you write to dealers who specialize in your field and also to some generalists who offer a wide range of materials. Eventually, you will develop a feel for the sources best suited to your collection.

Aside from a common area of specialization, a dealer's prices are very important to you. The price guide in the back of this book should be helpful in giving you a general feel for the prices of many autographs, but sending to dealers for their catalogs will prove even more useful. The most important factor in choosing a dealer is price consistency. You should be wary of the dealer who seems to offer a few autographs at bargain prices and many others at very high, unreasonable prices. The consistent dealers are the dealers who know pricing and, in my opinion, they are the most honest. They are not trying to give the appearance of reasonable prices by offering a few bargains and overpricing the rest of the material. Once you receive the catalogs of many dealers, including those well-known in the hobby and those who are just starting, you will notice quite a few differences in their prices. When you patronize an experienced, well-established dealer, you are paying not only for the autograph, but for his expert judgment of whether the material being sold is authentic. Inexperienced dealers must sell material for less money than established dealers until they build a similar reputation, or otherwise no one will buy from them. My general advice to collectors regarding whom to buy from depends upon their level of experience. If someone has been around for awhile and has learned how to authenticate autographs on his or her own, I often recommend dealers who, although reputable and honest, are inexpensive. I usually refer the novice collector to a more experienced dealer. Once you become a knowledgeable collector, you should be able to buy items from inexperienced people and not be afraid to trust your assessment of the material.

You might also be interested in discovering for yourself those dealers who are the most helpful, and who have the most expertise in authenticating autographs. Many dealers will cooperate with the collector — there is a lot of competition in the field — and will gladly look at copies of autographs you send them. Be sure to enclose a self-addressed, stamped envelope for their reply. By sending copies of some of your autographs to various dealers for comment, you can then select the dealers who are the most knowledgeable and the most willing to help you make the best purchases.

Whether buying at auctions or from autograph dealers, remember to be wary of inexperienced dealers or dealers who are not at least members of the UACC or The Manuscript Society. It's a good idea to solicit catalogs from a number of sources and to keep them on file so that you can cross-reference prices. If you take the time to search out reputable dealers who are experts in your field, you will eventually possess a collection made up of unquestionably genuine material at the least cost.

Signed portrait photograph of Bette Davis, **$15.**

3

Collecting Autographs Through the Mail

An inexpensive way to acquire a large, interesting, and valuable collection of autographs is to write to famous personalities requesting their signatures. Initially this may not seem to be the easy task it actually is. After all, you first have to find a workable address for the celebrity whose autograph you desire. You may also have difficulty writing a letter that will achieve the desired result. Or, you may have trouble discovering whether the autographs you receive are authentic or are machine, secretarial, or rubber-stamped signatures. Yet, these difficulties are all easy to overcome. In a period of five years, I collected over one thousand authentic autographs through the mail without devoting more than two or three hours per week to the task. Hundreds of other collectors have done the same thing.

Collecting autographs through the mail is the best way to "invest" in autographs, since it requires a limited financial outlay on your part. For example, in 1976, a collector wrote to

Jimmy Carter, who was on the campaign trail at the time, and asked him to define his defense policy. Carter's handwritten reply, which cost the collector only postage, could have been sold for $1,500. Although this is an extreme example, sending two, good quality, black-and-white photographs to a famous personality in almost any area of achievement, with a self-addressed, stamped envelope for their return, costs about $5. One photograph, if authentically signed, could be sold anywhere from $8 to $15 or more, depending upon the celebrity; the other could be added to your collection. By doing this, you can make money and expand your collection at the same time. How to sell these duplicates and other aspects of selling your collection are covered in chapter 10.

The average autograph collector spends most of his or her time collecting autographs through the mail and rounds out the collection by buying autographs as necessary to build a

Italian film director Federico Fellini, **$15.**

more extensive or historical representation. It is also possible to collect autographs in person if you live in such cities as New York, Los Angeles, or Washington, D.C., where famous people are easily found.

The first problem in writing to famous personalities is finding workable addresses. Most of the failures that collectors experience in writing away for autographs are the result of bad addresses. However, good, workable addresses are not as hard to locate as you might think, and you can find many on your own. All congressmen and senators can be written to in care of their Senate or Congressional offices in Washington, D.C. Books at your local library, such as *Who's Who in America, The International Who's Who, Who's Who in American Politics, Current Biography,* and similar works,

French actress Annabella, **$10.**

German World War II ace Erich Hartmann, **$15.**

list the addresses (sometimes even home addresses) of authors, politicians, astronauts, and many others. Current baseball, football, hockey or basketball players can be written to in care of their teams. Usually, the name of the stadium and the city is enough information to get the letter to them. Retired Hall of Fame members in these sports can be reached by way of their respective Halls of Fame. All authors can be written to in care of their publishers, and all astronauts can be reached via NASA, at the Johnson Space Center, Houston, Texas. Cartoonists, whose strips appear in your daily paper, can be addressed in care of the syndicators of their strips. These are identified in the strip, and the addresses of the syndicators can be found in *Editor and Publisher* magazine, available at your local library. Good addresses for movie and TV stars are more difficult to locate. Writing to the television or movie studios is seldom successful because the stars are besieged with fan mail through these addresses. One good way to reach the stars is through the Los Angeles area phone book (also available in the library). Many stars have set up production companies for themselves, such as Burt Reynolds Productions, and these addresses can be found in the Yellow Pages. These production companies are much smaller than the studios and you have a better chance of having your letter reach the personality. In addition, letters addressed to stars in care of their agents will usually be forwarded to the star.

Although these sources can help you acquire many autographs, they are not always productive. Most list business or agency addresses, and, in some cases, the offices will forward the letter to the personality's home address. However, a letter sent to a celebrity's home is more direct and effective.

Another problem you might face by using some of these sources is the chance of not receiving authentic autographs in return. For example, instead of forwarding your letters, sometimes the agencies or organizations you contact will send you printed facsimiles, machine signatures, secretarial examples, or rubber stamps instead. Baseball stadiums often send pictures of the players with an unauthentic signature printed on the photograph. Writing to senators or astronauts in care of their offices or

NASA will sometimes elicit a machine signature on a form letter or photograph. Writing to movie stars through studios or production companies, or even at home, can produce a secretarial or rubber-stamped autograph in return. There are also "fan mail services" that answer the mail and sign autographs for many movie stars.

The problem can be solved by using home addresses. This does not guarantee that you will obtain the autograph, nor does it guarantee that the autograph will be genuine. But it improves your chances tremendously. Also, home addresses are relatively easy to locate, but you won't be able to find them on your own and will have to purchase them instead. Home addresses of personalities in virtually all fields are found in *The Pen and Quill* and *Newsreel Magazine,* both of which are autograph publications; in address books, such as Roger Christensen's *Ultimate Movie, TV, and Rock Directory;* and from lists sold by individuals and firms. The prices range from lists that sell addresses for pennies each up to firms that charge about fifty cents per address. Some lists and firms are better than others. The best sources of addresses, whether they are published in magazines, books or lists, sold in bulk or individually, are listed in the back of this book. There are so many home address sources in the hobby that, after perusing a few lists, you'll find that you can locate the home address of virtually anyone.

Once you have found the address of the person you wish to contact for an autograph, your next step is to compose a letter that will bring you success. There are a few general guidelines that should increase your chance of getting the autograph. First and foremost, *ask* for the autograph, never demand one. Some people feel that celebrities have a duty to sign autographs because their fans put them where they are. Even if this were true, it is, nevertheless, not a good way to further your chance of success. Also, as an act of courtesy to the celebrity and as a means to improve your success rate, always enclose a self-addressed, stamped envelope with your letter. Many of the personalities you write to (such as retired, old film stars) are not wealthy and the cost of sending autographs can be prohibitive if the person receives many requests. Make sure that the self-addressed, stamped envelope is the proper size and bears the correct postage to guarantee the return of the material to you. The people at the Post Office are always glad to tell you how much money you will need to mail certain items. Another important act of courtesy is to never send more than two or three items for the person to sign. Remember, there are many other people besides yourself who are writing to the same celebrities. These celebrities have a limited amount of time to answer their autograph requests. If you send too many items, your request might go unanswered.

When writing your request letter, try to make it as neat as possible. If at all possible, type it, unless you have very neat and legible handwriting. You won't get the autograph if your request letter can't be deciphered. Typing lends seriousness to the request and will further your chance of obtaining an authentic autograph. Your letter should not be too long (because the celebrity is busy), but it should also not be as brief as the following:

> Dear Celebrity,
>
> Please send me your autograph on the enclosed card.
>
> Thank you,
>
> *John Jones*
>
> John Jones, Collector

You have a much better chance of obtaining the autograph if your letter is sincere and informs the celebrity why you want their autograph, why you admire them, and so forth. A personal touch to your letter is also a good idea. Tell the celebrity a little bit (not too much!) about yourself. You might want to add a personal touch in another way. For example, if you are writing to a military leader, and you served indirectly under his command, mention it in the letter. If you are writing to a news commentator, mention that you watch his or her broadcast and on what channel. Mention the movie you just saw or the colorful career he or she has had if you are writing to an actor or actress. If there is some particular relationship to a hometown, school, or business, mention it. But no matter what approach you use, remember that it is most important to be courteous, respectful, and sincere, and to enclose an appropriately sized, self-addressed, stamped envelope.

Sometimes you will be writing an autograph request letter to someone whom you do not admire, but nevertheless want their autograph for your collection. In this case, you don't have to lie and say that you are an admirer of the person, but you should be tactful. You might want to phrase the letter something like the following.

Dear Mr. Jones,

I am a collector of autographs of famous and important politicians. Would you please be so kind as to sign the enclosed photograph and mail it back to me in the enclosed, stamped envelope?

Thank you very much,

Bill Smith

Bill Smith, Collector

This letter shows respect for the person, and yet it says nothing of whether the writer likes them or not. Avoid lying at all costs. You are not dealing with stupid people. Celebrities receive many requests, and they will see through yours if it is insincere. Never make up stories about your "illness" or "blindness" or your "fatal disease" to try to trick the celebrity into giving you an autograph. It seldom works, and can backfire.

Virtually anything can be sent to celebrities through the mails for their signatures. In addition to 3x5 file cards, First Day Covers, available through the Post Office, are nice to have signed, especially if the stamp coincides with the celebrity's field. A Babe Ruth stamp cover autographed by a modern-day ballplayer is a good example. Photographs, record albums, and posters are excellent choices too. But make it easy for the celebrity to return the item to you. Don't forget the appropriately sized, self-addressed, stamped envelope. It is true that many celebrities will send you free photographs and other items if you request them (and enclose an SASE), and lists

of these celebrities are printed in the various autograph magazines. However, unless you are sure that a celebrity does not mind sending free photographs, always provide the items to be signed and this should help your success rate.

Sending request letters and material to celebrities in foreign countries is not difficult. You can obtain International Reply Coupons at the Post Office to include with your letter. The celebrity, in turn, can trade these in for return postage. The Post Office will tell you how many coupons you will need for various sized packages and envelopes.

You might wish to try for interesting autograph combinations through the mail, such as sending a Babe Ruth First Day Cover to five or ten of your favorite baseball players, or a photograph of Ronald Reagan and George Bush together for each of them to sign. However, when trying to get more than one autograph on an item, you do risk losing the item or photograph altogether. For example, unless you can get a senator or congressman to obtain it for you, it is impossible to get an authentic autograph of a current president through the mail.

Many people simply do not sign autographs through the mail no matter how nice your letter is. Others will sign only under certain circumstances, or only for those fans who write the best letters. People who do not readily respond to autograph requests are listed in various autograph magazines. It might be a good idea for you to obtain these publications (listed at the end of the book) or else correspond with other collectors regarding those they consider a risk to photographs or postage money. However, if you want an autograph badly enough, you may want to persist, as almost everyone

WARNER BROS.

Warner Bros. Inc.
4000 Warner Boulevard
Burbank, California 91522
213 843 6000
Cable Address: Warbros

September 9, 1980

Mr. Bob Bennett
One Governor's Lane
Shelburne, VT   05482

Dear Mr. Bennett,

Thank you for your very complimentary letter
of recent date. It is always great to hear that
people enjoy our cartoons.

As you may be aware, Warner Bros. Cartoons is
starting full-scale production of cartoons again.
We are currently enlarging and expanding our department. Due to our hectic production schedule, however,
I am unable to honor your request for a cartoon sketch.

Enclosed please find the autographed card you
requested. Best of luck in your endeavors.

Sincerely,

Friz Freleng
Senior Executive Producer

FF:kh

Enclosure: 1

Letter signed by animator Friz Freleng noting that he is unable to send a sketch, **$10.**

New York, N.Y.
August 23, 1980

Dear Mr. Bennett:

Thank you so much for your

lovely letter. I'm so glad you like

Tippie, and I'm happy to enclose the

autographs you requested for your

collection, including Tippie's, of

course.

With my very best wishes to

you,

Sincerely

Edwina

100 W. 57th St.
New York, N.Y.
10019

Cartoonist Edwina Dumm, now retired, graciously included an "autograph" of Tippie (see chapter 7) with this letter, **$5.**

will sign under the right set of circumstances. Related to this problem is the problem of unauthentic autographs — celebrities who have machines, secretaries, or rubber stamps to sign autographs for them. One method of getting reluctant signers to answer your letter or to avoid unauthentic autographs, is to stress in your letter that you are a serious autograph collector. You could tell the celebrity about other important autographs in your collection and mention that you are assembling a collection you hope will be historically important, so authenticity is a must. Many celebrities feel so flattered that their autograph will be part of a select group of authentic material, they will comply with your request. Of course, the only way to prove that the autograph is genuine is to compare it with other genuine specimens. You might even politely request that the celebrity return your material unsigned if they are unable or unwilling to personally sign it. Another

Double photographs of film stars make nice display items. Marlene Dietrich and Shirley Temple, **$35.**

Laurence Olivier and Joan Fontaine, **$50.**

Faye Dunaway and Helen Slater, **$20.**

suggestion for obtaining the autographs of reluctant signers, or retrieving material from celebrities who have kept items sent to be signed for several months, is the follow-up letter. This is simply a polite note to the celebrity explaining that you have not yet received the autograph and asking if he or she would please try to send it in the near future. The follow-up letter shows that you are serious about obtaining the autograph and this action often brings results. Many celebrities do not bother to sign until they receive a follow-up letter.

Besides writing to celebrities to obtain their simple signatures or signed photographs, you might also try to generate more interesting and unusual responses. A collection can become much more exciting if it contains material such as double-signed photos, signed original sketches of cartoonists, and handwritten or typed letters from celebrities in response to written questions you have submitted.

Mae Clarke and James Cagney, **$50.**

Instead of just asking for an autograph, you might try asking celebrities something about their careers or their new projects, or thoughts on a specific topic. The most valuable additions to your collection can be acquired in this manner, although obtaining these exciting items is not easy. Since many celebrities often do not have the time to answer your questions with a long answer, you must make your requests interesting and challenging. This tease will sometimes provoke results. To do this, go to the library and research the person whose autograph you desire and familiarize yourself with his or her work and achievements. Next, prepare an interesting and original question to ask your subject — one they will enjoy answering. Otherwise, they probably won't bother with it. You must use your imagination to formulate good questions, but, if you are clever, you may be rewarded by thoughtful responses.

Some examples of general questions you might ask include those about their educational training, or their advice to someone who wanted to enter their profession. Politicians might respond to a question on a local or national issue. You might want to ask a cartoonist where the inspiration came for a character. Or, ask a sports player how he felt when he achieved some milestone. How did Pete Rose feel when he recorded base hit number four thousand? Actors and actresses might enjoy discussing their favorite film and why it was their favorite. Or, dare to be more specific and ask questions of greater depth than those suggested here.

If you aren't interested in asking questions, but still want to obtain some valuable, exciting items, try sending an author a typed quote from his book to sign, or asking your favorite composer to write a few lines or

notes from one of his songs and sign it. Cartoonists are usually willing to make you an original sketch of their characters, and you might also try asking any celebrity to do a quick self-portrait for you. The possibilities are really endless. There are hundreds of types of autographs you can obtain, including letters, documents, signed quotes, photographs, or artwork. Just remember to use your imagination, be courteous and respectful to the celebrity, and thank them in advance for their kindness. You can use the mail to obtain many worthwhile and important items for your collection.

Self-portrait of poet Allen Ginsberg, **$15.**

4

Areas in Which to Collect

Once you start your autograph collection, you will quickly realize that you can't collect everyone's autograph. You could collect at random, but to build a serious collection, you should specialize in one or a few areas. Even if you do specialize, you will find that the possibilities within a given field are limitless, and you may want to again select limits within your chosen field. For example, suppose that you collect movie star autographs. There are thousands of movie stars of the past and present, major and minor. You certainly won't be able to get autographs from them all, because many are difficult to find and others are terribly expensive. So within the field of movie stars, you might find that specializing in Academy Award winners, "Tarzan" actors, or cast members is best for you. Collecting at random has two major problems. First, you won't assemble an in-depth collection in a specific area, and, since your collection contains personalities from many fields, it will lack exclusiveness. You'll have mostly what everyone else has. The other problem is that each

Signed photograph of early rock and blues musician, "Fats" Domino, **$20.**

field demands its own form of collecting savvy. For example, when you are collecting movie stars, you need to know more about secretarial signatures than machine signatures, but the opposite is true when you are collecting astronauts.

41

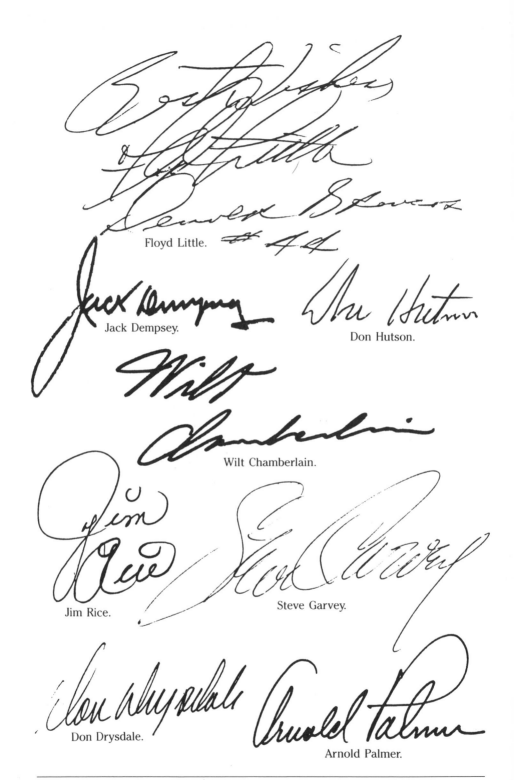

Floyd Little.

Jack Dempsey.

Don Hutson.

Wilt Chamberlain.

Jim Rice.

Steve Garvey.

Don Drysdale.

Arnold Palmer.

Signatures of these sports players range in value from **$3 to $5.**

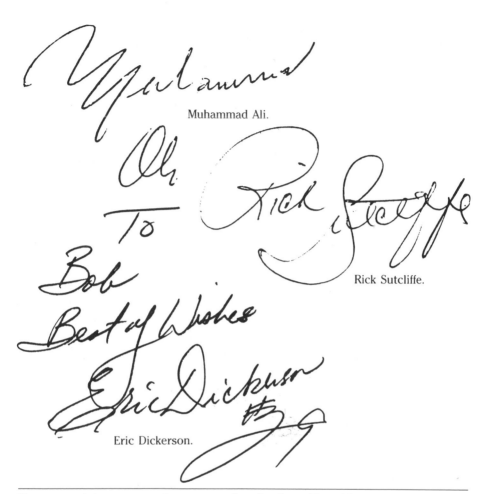

Muhammad Ali.

Rick Sutcliffe.

Eric Dickerson.

Signatures of these sports players range in value from **$3 to $5.**

There are countless areas from which to collect, some more difficult than others, and some that offer better investment opportunities. Autograph collectors have specialized in such diverse areas as politicians, film stars, sports stars, authors, poets, scientists, astronauts, Supreme Court justices, royalty, famous women, military leaders, Nobel Prize winners, world leaders, musicians, religious leaders, cabinet members, cartoonists, balloonists, stamp designers, models, and *Titantic* survivors. And there are many others that might be of interest to you.

We will explore the merits and some of the difficulties of various collecting categories in later chapters. Remember, that it is important to stick with a few areas and avoid collecting randomly. But don't stop yourself from getting someone's autograph whom you admire just because they aren't in your field. Try to concentrate your major efforts in your field or fields, but don't feel that you are making a grievous error when you occasionally step outside your area of specialty.

It is also not a good idea to go too deeply into your field. For example, if

Roger Moore, **$15.**

you are collecting baseball players, collect people like Ted Williams, Babe Ruth, Pete Rose, and Willie Mays rather than Ray Oyler, Choo Choo Coleman, Pumpsie Green, and Sibbi Sisti. If you choose the movie star area, stay with Burt Reynolds, Elizabeth Taylor, and Clint Eastwood rather than John Agar, Vera Hruba Ralston, and Sonny Tufts. If you have a personal attachment to some of the lesser lights in your specialization, go ahead and collect them, but don't expect them to become very valuable.

To help decide what your specialty should be, ask yourself two questions. The first question is: "Does my field offer opportunities for making money with autographs?" The second question is: "Does my field interest me personally?"

Harrison Ford, **$25.**

Jessica Lange, **$15.**

Debra Winger, **$15.**

Phoebe Cates, **$15.**

Bill Terry (Baseball Hall of Fame), **$10.**

Burleigh Grimes (also Baseball Hall of Fame), **$10.**

Many people collect autographs for only the fun of it. This is fine, but if you are concerned with investment possibilities, your choice of specialization is very important. Virtually every field offers some financial opportunity, but some fields are more profit-oriented than others. The highest quality items from the people of greatest achievement or fame in their field are always the best choices within a given area. Although they require more investment money on your part, historical autographs probably offer the best profit potential. Note that many historical autographs are in existence that never have had tremendous value and what little they do possess might even decrease in value. For example, unless you want to complete a collection of presidents, you probably won't want the autograph of Millard Fillmore or Franklin Pierce. Unless their signatures are on historically important letters or documents, which is unlikely in both of their cases, the value would be low. Simple signatures of these two might even decrease in value in the coming years. Aside from historical autographs, the autographs of astronauts, scientists, and Nobel Prize winners offer exciting possibilities if the individuals collected have achieved a great measure of fame, and the items collected are important, historically or otherwise. The autographs of politicians who may one day become presidents, vice-presidents, or Supreme Court justices, are worthy investments, but the autographs of the average senator or representative are not. The autographs of lesser-known senators and representatives from the nineteenth century are worth little more, and sometimes less, than the autographs of today's senators and representatives.

Bill Sturm (animator), sketch from the 1939 feature cartoon *Gulliver's Travels,* **$12.**

Berke Breathed sketch from "Bloom County" (© 1985 Washington Post Writers Group. Printed with permission), **$10.**

Terry Gilliam (character from "Monty Python)," **$10.**

Often overlooked by many serious autograph collectors and dealers are autographs of current artists, musicians, writers, etc. Collectors and dealers spend a great deal of time collecting great authors, painters, sculptors, and classical musicians, as well as other representatives of the fine arts. These are, of course, fine investment items if they are of good quality. Yet, those same collectors overlook items of popular art and culture of the recent past and present. It is true that many popular culture celebrities are only passing fancies forgotten in a short period of time, but this only means that you have to be more careful in your selections. Remember, demand is the most important factor in the price of an autograph. With this in mind, consider how many more people have heard of

Eldon Dedini, **$8.**

Ralph Bakshi (animator), self-portrait,
$10.

Charlie Chaplin than of John Tyler (U.S. president), Stuart O. Roosa (astronaut), or Clyde Tombaugh (discoverer of the planet Pluto). Many individuals in the movies, popular art, cartoon art, sports, and popular music fields are going to become or have already become legends. They will be remembered far longer than Tyler, Roosa, or Tombaugh. The point here is that more people would rather have a signed photograph of Charlie Chaplin, for whatever reasons, than one of any of the other individuals. Chaplin is a better investment. In the movie field people such as Chaplin, John Wayne, Clark Gable, and Marilyn Monroe will be remembered for many years, while obscure politicians or scientists will be long forgotten. In sports, Babe Ruth, Lou Gehrig, and Red Grange will be famous for years to come, and their placement in the Hall of Fame guarantees this fact. Cartoonists and animators will likely be forgotten in most cases, but their characters will live on. Think of the cultural importance of a sketch of Mickey Mouse by Walt Disney or a Disney animator, or even a sketch of Felix the Cat by animator

Otto Messmer. I believe that these characters have become a permanent part of American culture. In popular music, singers of the 1950s and 1960s, such as Chuck Berry and Bob Dylan, have already become legendary. Popular culture autographs are tremendous bets for appreciation. These living legends are well worth the effort of a carefully written autograph request and the cost of the postage. Once again, the challenge comes with

Pat Oliphant (political cartoonist), sketch of Jimmy Carter, **$10.**

August 3, 1979

Dear Mr. and Mrs. Miglis:

Mrs. Nixon and I join in this expression of our heartfelt congratulations as you reach the very special milestone of celebrating your Sixtieth Wedding Anniversary on August the tenth.

With our very best wishes and the hope that it may be the happiest of occasions for you and your family,

Sincerely,

(signature)

Mr. and Mrs. Frank Miglis
c/o Bob Bennett
1 Governor's Lane
Shelburne, Vermont 05482

Signed letter, from the inside of a card showing his California home, by Richard Nixon, **$65**.

separating the fads from the potential legends. In my opinion balloonists, stamp designers, and *Playboy* playmates (unless they become famous like Marilyn Monroe) have virtually no investment potential.

The secret of accumulating a first-class autograph collection is preparation. Choose your special area within the framework of your knowledge and interests. I think that it's a good idea to have at least an informal outline of your goals, not forgetting complementary sub-areas, before you begin to collect. Eventually, you will become more knowledgeable and secure in your own judgments. Then you can round out and fine-tune the collection.

This periodic reassessment is absolutely essential. You'll no doubt be pleasantly surprised at the distance you have covered, but this is also a good time to upgrade the collection by trading, selling, or making a judicious purchase. You might wish to review your goals at this time. With knowledge and expertise comes a higher level of sophistication, so this may be the time to expand your horizons. Whatever shape these decisions take, your investment of time and money should only increase the satisfaction and financial value you will realize from your autograph collection.

5

Historical Autographs and Documents

John Quincy Adams, **$125.**

Andrew Jackson, **$300.**

Ronald Reagan, **$75.**

Lyndon Johnson, **$125.**

The autographs of history's great names on letters, documents, manuscripts, and photographs is the longest established and most respected area of specialization in the hobby of collecting autographs. Aside from movie stars, where signatures from secretaries and other forgeries abound, it is also one of the trickiest fields. Oftentimes the authentication of historical material involves matching inks and papers and uncovering the work of ancient forgers. Yet, collecting historical autographs can be very exciting if you enjoy this detective work. Historical autographs are generally the most valuable, and their worth has been well established for many years. They are relatively safe investments because their value has withstood the test of time. One drawback, however, is the difficulty of finding these items, which all carry very high price tags. This can place them out of the reach of many collectors. Still, some of the

Woodrow Wilson

THE WHITE HOUSE
WASHINGTON

Woodrow Wilson, **$100.**

Dwight D. Eisenhower

Dwight D. Eisenhower, **$150.**

Abraham Lincoln

Abraham Lincoln, **$1,000.**

Franklin D. Roosevelt

Franklin D. Roosevelt, **$275.**

minor individuals of the past can be obtained reasonably, and if you specialize, your historical collection could become very valuable.

There are many, many types of historical autographs to collect, almost all of which possess great value. Among these are authors, scientists, inventors, politicians, artists, composers, royalty, military leaders, religious leaders, and many others. And, of course, many sub-fields exist within each category. Under the heading of politicians, autographs of presidents, or signers of the Declaration of Independence, or prominent members of either party during a given time frame are possibilities. Because these autographs can be expensive, it is more important to specialize within this category than with any other autograph field. There are simply thousands and thousands of historical autographs that can be collected, but collecting at random will not further the value of your collection as a whole. If you wish to buy a few historical autographs for investment purposes, you probably do not need to specialize. Or, if your primary interest falls in a different area, such as sports, but you would like to own a few historical autographs, don't shy away from collecting them. But, if building a valuable and extensive historical collection is your goal, you must specialize.

Oscar Wilde

Oscar Wilde, **$150.**

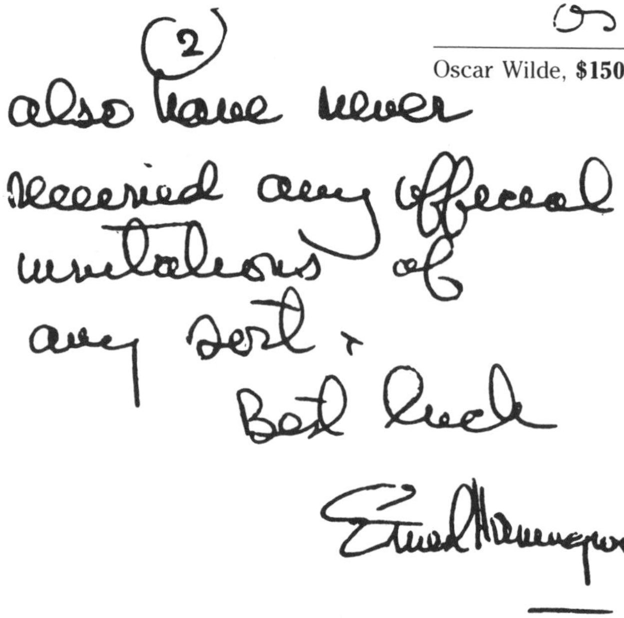

also have never
received any official
invitations of
any sort —
    Best Luck

    Ernest Hemingway

Ernest Hemingway, A.N.S., **$250.**

F Scott Fitzgerald

F. Scott Fitzgerald, **$100.**

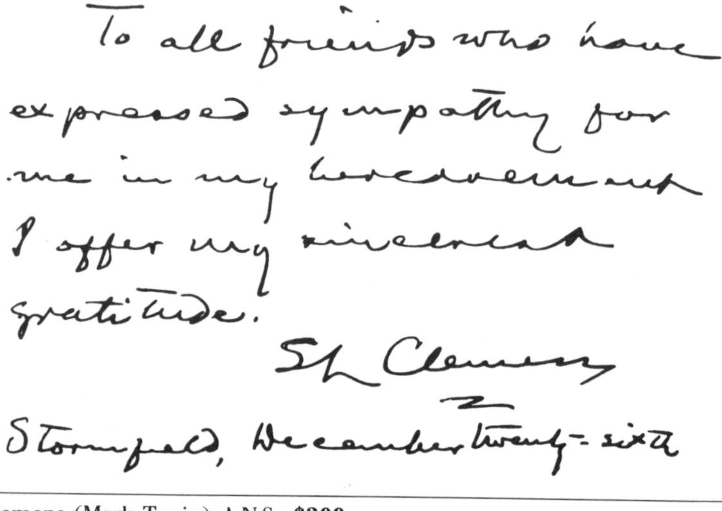

To all friends who have
expressed sympathy for
me in my bereavement
I offer my sincerest
gratitude.
    SL Clemens
Stormfield, December twenty-sixth

Samuel Clemens (Mark Twain) A.N.S., **$300.**

54

John Bright (British influence on American politics), **$15.**

Wendell Phillips (abolitionist), **$10.**

Robert G. Ingersoll (lecturer), **$20.**

Thomas Bayard (politician), **$10.**

The best way to collect historical autographs is to choose a subject dear to you and then narrow that field into one or more small, manageable areas.

Using my own historical collection as an example, let me show you how this works for me. I am interested in American history, especially the study of what I perceive to be the American political tradition — the ideas of the Declaration of Independence carried through the American political experience. Some of the individuals and movements that I collect fit loosely within this framework, but that doesn't matter, because the collection makes sense to me and holds together in some manner. I collect people such as Jefferson, Paine, and other Founding Fathers; Ralph Waldo Emerson, Henry David Thoreau and Walt Whitman, Harriet Beecher Stowe and other abolitionists; classical liberals, and even anarchists. Autographs of the Founding Fathers and people such as Thoreau and Whitman are expensive, so I also collect less costly material in my field. For instance, a signature of abolitionist Wendell Phillips can be purchased for $10. Alone, it is not very valuable, but, taken with the rest of my collection, it becomes more valuable because the total value of the collection is increased. Similar things can be done in other fields. For example, if you collect authors, you might limit yourself to those of the Romantic era. You simply must specialize when collecting historical material unless you have the funds to obtain everyone. Your collection will also be more satisfying and valuable if you frame it in an interesting context.

Signed photograph of President Jimmy Carter, **$75.**

There are many other things to keep in mind when you are collecting historical material. Historical autographs are very rare and scarce, and because of this, you are not likely to find some of the items you want immediately. It might take you a few years before a letter or even a signature of George Washington becomes available. In order to start your collection, you must contact many dealers and sellers of autographs and find out what is available to you at the present time. Don't waste time waiting and waiting for an autograph that you may never have the chance to purchase. There are thousands of other interesting historical personalities to select in the meantime. Search out other pertinent material in your field and purchase it. In this way you will begin to define your collection much as I did.

Also related to scarcity is the fact that a great deal of the historical material in private hands is being purchased by public institutions and museums. Because of this, if you do come across an authentic autograph of George Washington, which fits into your collection, purchase it if at all possible. Such a rare autograph can always be re-sold for at least the price you paid for it, if it was purchased from a reputable seller.

You might be tempted to collect some of the less well-known individuals in a given area since the prominent names are rare and expensive. As we stated when discussing specialization, the total value of your collection can be enhanced by filling it out with lesser-known personalities. However, if you purchase less well-known people outside your area of specialty, you might have trouble selling those autographs at a later time. For example, you might wish to purchase a signature of former senator and President Grover Cleveland's secretary of state, Thomas Bayard, for your collection of nineteenth century senatorial autographs or nineteenth century Democrats. But if you bought this item for no particular reason, you could have trouble selling it later, unless you found a nineteenth century collector. Big names such as Washington and Lincoln are easily sold; lesser lights, such as Bayard, are not.

When buying historical autographs, price usually depends upon the type and condition of the item, to a greater degree than with any other type of autograph. But the historical importance of a letter or document is such a major factor in price that even letters from unknowns or lesser-known individuals, such as Civil War soldiers writing letters describing a battle, can command high price tags. Signed photographs, particularly if the photographs are old or have value in and of themselves, are also widely sought and are usually more interesting and valuable than letters from famous personalities on unimportant subjects.

Photographs are also more attractive as display pieces than most letters or documents, which also gives them value. M. Wesley Marans, a collector of photographs signed by historical personalities, has put together a beautiful book illustrating his collection entitled, *Sincerely Yours* (1983). The photographs reprinted in the work show the tremendous depth that a collection of signed photographs can have. It contains great names of history at leisure or work, in photographic portraits or snapshots that are interesting and exciting to see on display.

Simple signatures of famous historical personalities are less valuable, but they should not be ignored, especially if you have limited financial resources. For example, a routine document signed by Abraham Lincoln is worth around $2,500 to $3,000, while a signature of Lincoln might be purchased for around $1,000. This signature could be matted and framed with a photograph or engraving of Lincoln, making a beautiful display piece. In and of themselves, signatures are not too attractive, but they are more versatile than larger, bulkier items. If you doubt the value of a simple signature, consider the fact that one from the pen of Shakespeare could be sold today for over one million dollars.

Condition is important with historical material, but there are many ways that damaged material can be repaired or made attractive in a display piece. Condition certainly affects the price of an item, but, if the item is of great importance, the value will not be significantly impaired. Inscriptions on photographs or signature slips do not lessen the value of historical material as they do with signed photographs or signatures from modern personalities such as movie stars. If your name is "Joe" you would be more likely to buy a signed photograph of Bo Derek without an inscription rather than one that read, "To Otis." However, historical material is of such great rarity that you are lucky to get it in any form, and you do not care if it is inscribed to

Claude DeBussy, **$200.**

Franz Liszt, **$200.**

Arturo Toscanini, **$150.**

George Gershwin signed musical
quotation, **$500.**

someone else. Another factor related to condition affecting the value of historical material is whether the item was signed in ink or pencil. Although pencil signatures become permanent after one hundred years or so, collectors still prefer items signed in ink. Ink signatures usually carry a higher price tag.

Framing and matting your historical autograph makes it more attractive as a display piece and enhances its value. We will look at how to do this in our chapter on preserving your collection.

Although virtually all historical autographs of well-known individuals are highly valued, there are a few unusual categories that offer both opportunity and danger for investment purposes. These categories include Nazis, criminals of the past such as Al Capone and Bonnie and Clyde, or outlaws such as Jesse James. Since many gangsters of the past have gained a certain romantic nostalgia, and people like Hitler have had a great impact upon history, these autographs are worth consideration. However, only the most notorious individuals in these areas should be perceived as good investments. The autographs of lesser Nazis or western gunmen might strengthen the collection as a whole, but, in and of themselves, are not too popular. Most people would not want an autograph of German General Von Ribbentrop hanging in their living room.

The best investments of all historical autographs are, in my view, those that represent scientific or cultural achievements of the past. Besides, the political category has very little to offer. Washington and Lincoln material is scarce and not many people want a James Polk signature or item. If you are interested in politics, you might want to collect people such as Adam Smith or Karl Marx whose ideas have had an impact on politics or economics. The autographs that are more culturally oriented are often better acquisitions, because prices in many cases are more reasonable, and because the popularity of individuals in these categories has withstood the test of time. Inventors and scientists have had tremendous influence on our lives, and the autographs of people such as Alexander Graham Bell and Thomas Edison are very worthy of collecting. Classical musicians like Bach and Beethoven have become legends, as have similar individuals in areas of literature, poetry, painting, and sculpture. Many people find a musical quotation signed by Franz Liszt much more exciting than a land grant signed by President James Monroe. Autographs of individuals who have had an impact upon culture are simply much more interesting to people than almost any other autographs, and should make both wonderful investments and enjoyable items to collect.

The greatest danger inherent in collecting historical autographs is the problem of forgery. Authentication of autographs by comparing signatures, which will be discussed later in the book, is not too difficult. Your task is usually much greater with forged material, since a knowledge of inks and papers is necessary to uncover forgery. The presence of forgeries of historical autographs makes it extremely necessary for you to purchase only from trusted dealers or to learn how to authenticate items yourself. Forgeries have caused many problems within the hobby and have even misled historians.

One of the greatest forgers of all time, Robert Spring, whose forgeries are worth at least $100 now because they are works of art, once forged a letter from Thomas Jefferson that detailed "Jefferson's plan" to cut taxes and halve the number of nationwide officeholders. This letter was examined by historians and scholars who labeled it authentic, yet autograph experts pronounced it to be a blatant Spring forgery. A forgery such as this could have caused historians to misinterpret some of the views or philosophy of Jefferson, so forgeries can be damaging to historical analysis.

The history of forgery is a very interesting and exciting one. Although forgeries have been very detrimental, collector Charles Hamilton correctly noted that forgeries add excitement to the hobby. Two of Hamilton's books, *Scribblers and Scoundrels* (1968) and *Great Forgers and Famous Fakes* (1980), offer entertaining accounts of

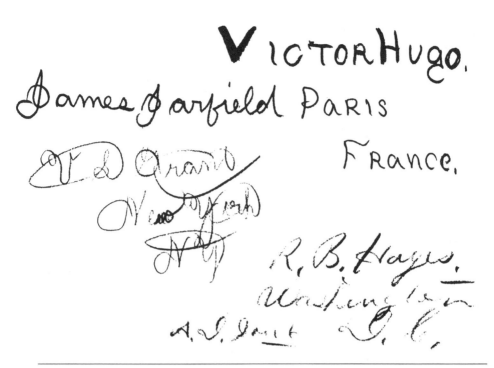

Crude collection of forgeries scrawled in an 1880s autograph album includes James Garfield, Victor Hugo, Ulysses S. Grant, and Rutherford B. Hayes.

forgers and forgeries. Stories about Clifford Irving, who forged Howard Hughes's will, and a seventeen-year-old boy, William Henry Ireland, who fooled many historians and literary experts with his forgeries of Shakespeare's signatures, are fascinating. Ireland's forgery of a new "Shakespeare" play finally brought his downfall. The two most famous historical forgers were Spring, who usually forged George Washington material, and Joseph Cosey, who forged Lincoln, Jefferson, Poe, and others. Although both were accomplished forgers, an autograph expert can readily identify their material.

There are several guidelines for identifying forgeries. Above all, don't let forgeries discourage you. If you were to ask a number of the biggest autograph dealers or experts how to identify a forgery, many would discourage you from trying to acquire this skill because of all of the problems with matching inks, papers, and so forth. You may have trouble with some of the better forgeries, but if you watch and learn a few simple things, you too can successfully identify them.

As stated previously, make sure you buy from a reputable dealer. Most forgeries are not purchased from the major dealers in the autograph hobby but at flea markets or from antiques dealers, or others who, although they might be honest, just don't know anything about autographs. Beware of bargains. Sometimes forgers will sell their ware cheaply because they want to get rid of it fast. Also, since forgers can easily turn out product, they don't need to wait for the *right* offer. In regard to reputability, you should never accept a statement of authenticity as proof that an autograph is genuine, unless it is issued by an expert autograph dealer or collector. Ignore statements of authenticity from relatives of the celebrity, associates of the celebrity, antiques dealers, or even the FBI. I recently had someone try to sell me some vintage movie star autographs that an FBI agent had looked over and pronounced as genuine (some were not, incidentally). With all respect to the FBI, FBI general agents simply do not know how to authenticate celebrity handwriting or other autographs. Statements of authenticity from some big official or authority might look good on paper, but unless they are autograph experts, the statement is as worthless as the forgery itself.

The best way to uncover a forgery is to compare the handwriting of the item you have with the documented handwriting of the person in question. Many books and pamphlets in the hobby offer facsimiles of the authentic autographs of historical personalities, and you should be able to find just about everyone. We will discuss how to proceed with your comparisons in chapter 8. Suspecting a forgery, however, you should look for handwriting that is unusually small, shaky, or has evidences of erasure. You should also beware of an unusual signature from a person. For example, if William Faulkner always signed his letters "Bill," you should treat a "William" signature more cautiously.

Also, it would be very useful for you to do some research on old inks and papers. Learn how to identify the differences between those of different time periods. This is not as difficult as it sounds. Early American documents are written in inks that seep into the paper and leave a slight browning at the edges of the writing. Forgeries often do not look like this old ink and have a washed out, brown appearance. If the ink appears "wrong" to you, treat the item with more caution. It is also important to be wary of someone offering you a very rare or important historical document. Virtually all such documents have already been found and are either in public hands, with private collectors, or in the possession of autograph dealers. There simply aren't many new discoveries.

As Charles Hamilton said in *Great Forgers and Famous Fakes* (1980), "A wholesome scepticism, a sharp mind and some knowledge of the facts behind a document will enable you to detect almost any forgery."

Besides forgeries, be aware that secretaries often signed for many historical personalities in all areas.

Adolf Hitler, **$200.**

Queen Victoria, **$125.**

Napoleon, **$400.**

Charles Lindbergh, **$250.**

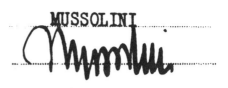

Benito Mussolini, **$150.**

Thomas Edison, **$100.**

Winston Churchill, **$200.**

Charles Darwin, **$300.**

Specifically, secretaries have signed for many American presidents, although these signatures are more likely to appear on land grants (almost always secretarials) and other insignificant items, rather than on important documents. One famous story showing the pervasiveness of secretarial signatures concerns President Franklin Roosevelt. Roosevelt once sent a check he signed to the bank to be cashed, but the bank refused to do so, claiming that it was not his authentic signature. The problem was that Roosevelt's secretary, Missy LeHand, usually signed his checks, and the bank noticed that the signatures didn't match. As with forgeries, comparison to authentic signatures will help you detect a secretarial signature. Forgeries and secretarials may impair the collection of historical autographs, but, if you are willing to learn about them, they will not be a significant roadblock in building an authentic collection.

6

Common Areas of Collecting

Many collectors who collect the autographs of modern personalities, living or deceased, are also interested in acquiring signatures in areas that are customarily categorized as historical material. These fields include authors, artists, sculptors, politicians, classical musicians, military and world leaders, businessmen and industrialists, as well as astronauts and Nobel Prize winners. There is no historical material existing of the last two categories, since both are relatively recent categories.

Several of the larger autograph firms handle personalities from these fields, and it is not too difficult to find the autograph of any senator, congressman, famous astronaut, or inventor, if you receive the catalogs of a few different dealers. These fields are perceived by many as *fine* autographs, and, therefore, are distinguished from popular autographs that include movie stars, popular musicians, cartoonists, and sports figures. While the autographs of politicians and world leaders, for instance, may not be the

General James Doolittle, **$15.**

good, overall investments as those of people in the movie category, political autographs (at least of the more important personalities) will eventually be classified as historical material and collected as such.

General Mark Clark, **$20.**

Most autographs of politicians and authors are collected on letters rather than on photographs as in the movie field. Letters written by senators discussing vital national issues are looked upon as being more important than a letter from a movie star discussing a new film. Similarly, most people would rather have a photograph signed by Bo Derek or Robert Redford on their walls than one signed by Tip O'Neill. When collecting the autographs of politicians, astronauts, and inventors through the mail, it is best to ask a question of the individual with the hope of eliciting a more significant treasure, such as a letter on an important topic. Signed quotations or manuscripts by authors can also be very valuable. Simple signatures of people in these fields have some value as well, but, if you are only interested in obtaining signatures, it would be wiser for you to collect autographs on First Day Covers that are related to the personality's area of achievement. For example, you could ask a senator or congressman (or several senators or congressmen) to sign a First Day Cover with a stamp honoring a president. Or you might request that a few world leaders autograph a cover bearing a stamp related to the United Nations or world peace. Nobel Prize inventors or scientists might be asked to sign a cover commemorating a great invention or inventor, such as Thomas Edison. If you are collecting simple signatures instead of important letters, signed quotations or manuscripts, keep in mind that First Day Covers are much more interesting and valuable than signed file cards, and more versatile as well. You might ask several people to sign the same cover in order to make a really attractive display piece. First Day Covers are available from many people who advertise in autograph publications, and also, of course, from the Postal Service.

If you write a well-written, informed letter to many of the personalities in the above fields, you stand a good chance of obtaining important and interesting responses to your queries. People such as politicians are always anxious to read their mail with the hope of gaining some insight into what their constituents are thinking. Inventors and scientists love to be lauded for their work, since many times it does not receive the recognition they believe it deserves.

One of the dangers in collecting the autographs of astronauts, politicians, and some of the other personalities we have mentioned, is the risk of receiving unauthentic autographs. The most common type of spurious autographs received from people in these fields are machine signatures. They are

Henry Kissinger.

G. Gordon Liddy.

Alf Landon.

Ted Kennedy.

Dean Rusk.

Spiro Agnew.

Ellsworth Bunker.

Clark Clifford.

Pictured examples, $5 to $10 each.

made by a machine called the "auto-pen," which has the ability (once a pen is inserted into it) to write a person's name exactly as he or she would sign it personally. With some practice, you should be able to spot an autopen signature quite easily, since the machine signs a person's name the same way every time, something no human being can do. To test this, try writing your name on two pieces of paper exactly the same way each time. Then, superimpose the papers and hold them over a lamp. You will see that it is just not possible for you to get every detail to match in both signatures. An autopen can.

Some celebrities try to fool collectors and others by using many different autopen patterns. Presidents usually have five or ten different patterns for different forms of their signature. Ronald Reagan uses a pattern for "Ron," "Ronald Reagan," and even "Dutch," for instance. If you keep track of the patterns published in many of the autograph magazines, you should be readily able to identify such signatures as autopens. An autopen also tends to write more uniformly than a person actually would. You'll see little or no speed variation or a difference in the weight of the pen-strokes within the signature. Finally, some autopen patterns wear out after many months, causing slight variations in signatures written months apart. Although this problem is not as big as it may sound, because the signatures will still be very close to each other, you can combat this by sending a celebrity more than one item to sign at the same time. You can match up the signatures yourself without having to wait for a pattern to appear in a magazine.

When collecting the autographs of politicians, it is especially important to concentrate only on the important names or on the people you think likely to become big names. History certainly has not been kind to all of the governors, senators, congressmen, and Supreme Court justices who have served over the years, not to mention some of our presidents. The problem is that many people do not know who their own congressman is, let alone the congressman from another district. They are far more likely to know the latest big movie star name or recording artist. In the political category, try to select people of presidential timbre, or those who become Supreme Court justices or garner some sort of influence or name recognition in Congress. Most senators and congressmen are willing to send out free, signed photographs or letters that answer your questions about issues. After all, they can send these to you at taxpayer expense. But, in many cases, these are signed by autopens, and every senator or congressman has access to one. You can usually obtain an authentic response if you ask them not to use the autopen. I once wrote back to a prominent congressman who had sent me an autopen-signed photograph and asked if he would please send a genuine autograph instead. He did so very graciously and enclosed a letter, also signed, asking what else he might do for me.

The major astronauts, especially people such as Neil Armstrong and Sally Ride, are usually receptive to autograph requests and answer questions that you ask of them. But again, you must be on the alert for the autopen. Autograph requests sent to NASA will almost always produce an

Neil Armstrong (authentic).

Alan Shepard.

Neil Armstrong (autopen, no value).

Gene Cernan.

Michael Collins.

Dave Scott.

Jim Irwin.

Charles Conrad.

Pictured examples, **$5 to $10 each.**

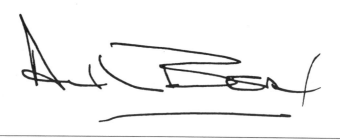

Alan Bean.

Buzz Aldrin.

D.K. Slayton.

Pictured examples, $5 to $10 each.

autopen signature. Because NASA receives so many requests it has a signature pattern for every astronaut in its files. If you send your request to an astronaut in care of NASA, ask that your letter be forwarded instead of answered by NASA, and specify in your letter that you do not want an autopen signature. Home or office addresses of astronauts are not hard to discover and are usually provided in autograph publications or address lists. As with all other autographs, this material is also readily available from dealers.

The United States government, and those individuals connected with it — politicians, astronauts, military leaders, etc. — are the biggest users of the autopen, since the machine is fairly expensive. Even former presidents such as Richard Nixon still use autopens, as well as secretaries, on occasion. So be careful, but remember

that some excellent autographs can be received from people in these areas. You might also consider collecting the signatures of important world leaders. The more famous world leaders are hard to obtain, but become very valuable in many instances. A few will answer your request letters through the mail if you write a polite and interesting letter. The autographs of people such as Fidel Castro, Arafat, and other notorious leaders are those that have proven to be the most valuable.

Since authors do a lot of writing, they are usually very willing to give autographs or to write a quotation from one of their works. They are easily written to in care of their publishers, and unauthentic autographs are not common. Authors are used to signing copies of their books, and,

ERICA JONG
author of the Signet paperback HOW TO SAVE YOUR OWN LIFE
Photo credit: Milton H. Greene

Signed photograph of author Erica Jong, **$15.**

Norman Mailer.

Peter Benchley.

Vincent Bugliosi.

Stephen King.

George Abbott.

Pictured examples, **$5 to $10 each.**

Roald Dahl.

Michael Crichton.

Robert Penn Warren.

Harold Robbins.

Kurt Vonnegut.

Pictured examples, **$5 to $10 each.**

Lowell Thomas.

29 May 1979

Isaac Asimov.

John Toland.

Ray Bradbury.

Pictured examples, **$5 to
$10 each.**

because of this, they don't seem to mind autographing. If you have an author's home address, it might be a good idea to send a copy of his or her book to sign. This will almost always prove successful if you remember to provide a properly stamped book mailer to save the author mailing expenses. You can write the author first asking him if he will sign the book for you if you send it, so that you won't lose the book. Some authors you might wish to contact include Isaac Asimov, Ray Bradbury, James Michener, Norman Mailer, Arthur Miller, James Dickey, or Allen Ginsberg. There are many fine literary personalities to write to and collect.

The fields of science and invention also offer interesting possibilities. You can build a collection of Nobel Prize winners, which can become very valuable, or just collect signed quotes or signatures of the more prominent in these fields. Some very interesting replies to your questions can be obtained from scientists and inventors. You might ask them to send you a quote about the work they are doing, their thoughts about the future of their field, or ask them to explain their invention or discoveries in simple terms. William Shockley, the scientist who was a co-inventor of the transistor, will send you a schematic drawing of the transistor signed by him, if you politely request one. John A. Wheeler, a physicist, will pen quotes about the future of his field for collectors. The discoverer of the planet Pluto, Clyde W. Tombaugh, graciously sends his autograph to collectors and adds the date that he discovered the planet as well. The point is, although you and others may have never heard of Shockley, Wheeler, or Tombaugh, their discoveries and their autographs are important and valuable. If you use your imagination to get something more than just a signature from a scientist or inventor, you can build a collection of really worthwhile items.

John A. Wheeler (A.Q.S.).

1981

John Kenneth Galbraith.

Alfred Hershey.

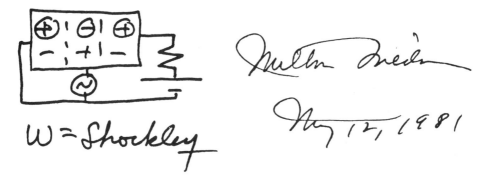

W = Shockley

William Shockley (with sketch of transistor, **$40.**

Milton Friedman.

Wernher von Braun, **$20.**

Linus Pauling.

Values **$5 to $10 each,** unless noted.

Classical musicians and popular singers and songwriters of the 1930s, 1940s and 1950s are also popular and easy to collect. Try asking these individuals to draw a musical quotation from one of their songs or works, or to write down some lyrics if they are lyricists. These items can become very valuable, especially if the songs have been very popular. Some of the musicians whom you might contact for autographs, or purchase from dealers, include Irving Berlin, Jascha Heifetz, Leonard Bernstein (who uses an autopen occasionally), Benny Goodman, Luciano Pavarotti, Burt Bacharach, John Williams, and many others. Unauthentic autographs are also not common in this field.

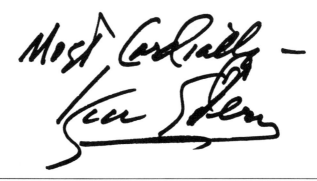

Isaac Stern.

Andre Kostelanetz.

Benny Goodman.

Pictured examples, **$5 to $10 each.**

74

Cab Calloway.

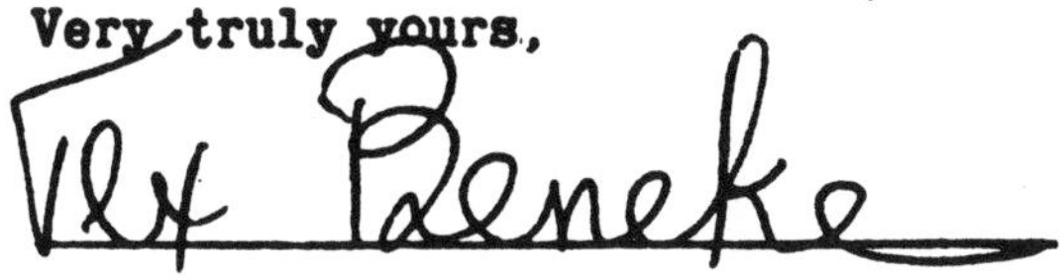

Very truly yours,

Tex Beneke.

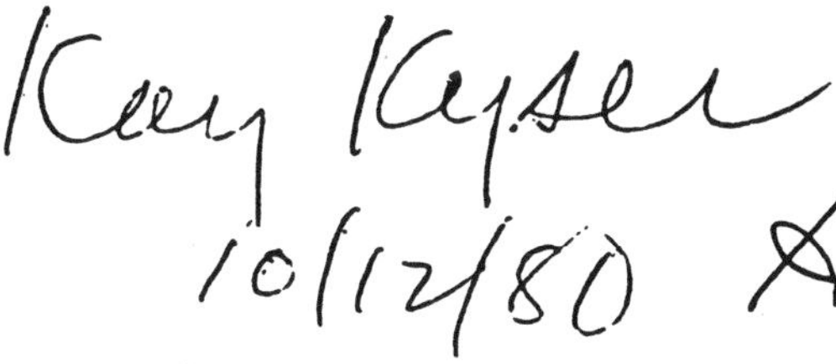

Kay Kyser.

10/12/80

Hoagy Carmichael.

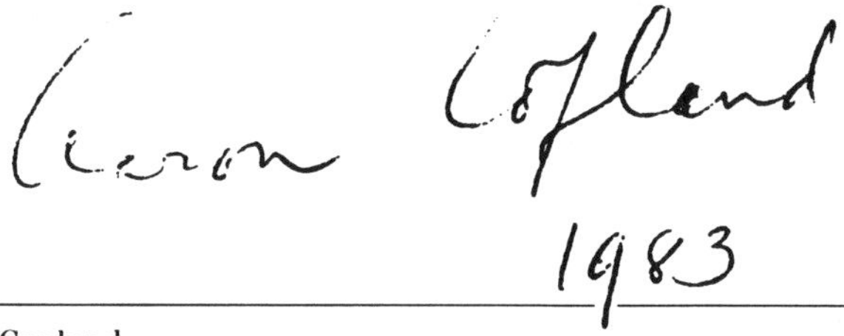

Aaron Copland.

1983

Harry James.

Pictured examples, **$5 to $10 each.**

Signed photograph of Nazi Albert Speer sent to collectors before his death. **$25.**

There are a few offbeat categories that are commonly collected, and these include Nazi personalities or World War II generals. Famous criminals are collected by a growing number of people. Several living Nazis or German World War II personalities send out autographs and pictures. Erich Hartmann, an ace, or Adolf Galland, a general, are two. Deceased Nazis' signatures can be purchased rather reasonably, depending upon the personality. Some collectors have taken historical events and collected all of the autographs related to it. An example is the atomic bombing of Hiroshima and Nagasaki in World War II. You can collect the autograph of Enola Gay pilot, Paul W. Tibbets, or several or all of the crew members. Addresses for these individuals are printed in address lists and "who's who" books, and unauthentic autographs are rare.

Some collectors are interested in the autographs of criminals such as Charles Manson and others. Although many dealers and collectors avoid involvement with this type of material, the autographs of some criminals have commanded very high prices. Manson's simple signatures sell for $50 and up at present. Obviously, it is for you to decide if you want to build a collection of this sort.

When collecting the autographs of politicians, scientists, authors, musicians, astronauts, world leaders, and others, try to remember that value is not always determined by the identity of the person who signed the autograph. Many of these individuals are not household names, although some have acquired great fame. Yet, an autograph connected to some important national issue, or to a famous invention or discovery, or to a popular song (even if the songwriter is not very famous), may add great value and excitement to your collection. Dealers will sell you these items for high prices, but autographs of many living personalities can be obtained for only the cost of postage.

"Pappy" Boyington.

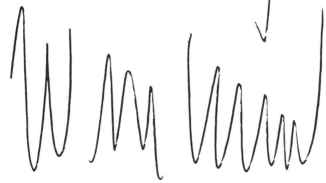

Hans Urich Rudel (Germany, WW II).

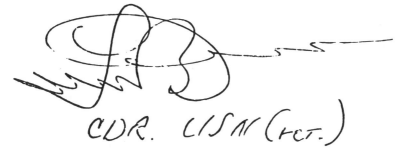

Lloyd Bucher.

William Westmoreland.

Paul Tibbets.

Pictured examples, **$5 to $10 each.**

Adolf Galland.

J. H. Doolittle.

October 19. 1981.

Sir Douglas Bader.

Autographed for Bob Bennett

M. B. Ridgway
General, US Army,
Retired

Matthew Ridgway.

Pictured examples, **$5 to
$10 each.**

7

Popular Autographs to Collect

In the 1950s and the 1960s, when autograph collecting began its first major growth in popularity, autographs of movie stars, sports stars, and popular musicians, were looked down upon by serious collectors and were perceived to have little or no value. This was partly due to the fact that most of the hobbyists at that time were collecting historical and literary material. They viewed those who collected movie stars and other popular autographs as "autograph hounds" who annoyed celebrities in restaurants or public places with autograph requests. Today, popular autographs have achieved and, in some cases, surpassed the value of many historical autographs. For example, a handwritten letter from Greta Garbo is equal in value to a letter written by Abraham Lincoln. A signed sketch of the character Garfield by creator Jim Davis is worth almost twice as much as a Ronald Reagan autograph. And a signature from the pen of Babe Ruth will sell for more than a signature of almost any American president.

There are two reasons for the tremendous growth in the value of popular autographs. One is the high level of inflation in the 1970s that, although it affected the prices of all autographs, jumped the prices of popular material to a serious level. The other reason is that many more people began collecting in the late 1960s and early 1970s, and these people chose to center their collection around movie stars or sports figures. The membership of the UACC in the mid-1960s was around 400, and most of the members specialized in historical material. At that time The Manuscript Society had more members than the UACC. Today, the UACC has about 2,000 members (more than The Manuscript Society), of which more than half collect popular autographs of some variety. This means that, although autographs of movie stars or sports figures have been collected for years (autograph albums from the 1920s and 1930s containing these signatures frequently appear on the market), collectors of popular

Fay Wray from *King Kong,* **$20.**

Elsa Lanchester from *The Bride of Frankenstein,* **$20.**

Olivia DeHavilland from *Gone with the Wind,* **$15.**

material have only recently become recognized as serious collectors of autographs. As we have discussed previously, popular autographs can be very good investments for the future. Personalities like Charlie Chaplin or Marilyn Monroe have acquired greater fame than the average senator or congressman. In short, they have become legendary figures. Since an autograph's value is based on the strength of consumer demand, the autographs of individuals who have acquired the greatest fame are generally more valuable than other autographs. This is not to say, however, that all popular autographs are worthy of collecting. One of the biggest dangers inherent in collecting popular material lies with collecting those individuals who are popular for only a short period of time and forgotten after a period of years. When collecting popular material, you must try to pick the winners. If you are able to do this, you can take pleasure in the thought that the personalities in your autograph collection have a good chance of becoming very valuable. The miracles of modern technology have made it possible for celebrities in the popular arts to become extremely well-known, and their autographs are recommended collectibles. As the noted collector Charles Hamilton wrote in his book, *The Signature of America* (1979), regarding the best autograph investments: "Collect presidents or signers [of the Declaration of Independence] if you wish, but I predict that during the next ten years the values of movie stars will increase faster than anything else in the area of philography."

Boris Karloff, **$75.**

Mary Pickford, **$20.**

Groucho (Marx), **$20.**

W. C. Fields, **$175.**

Sal Mineo, **$35.**

Henry Fonda, **$20.**

Basil Rathbone, **$70.**

Natalie Wood, **$20.**

Very truly yours,

X

JUDY GARLAND

Address:

Judy Garland, **$150.**

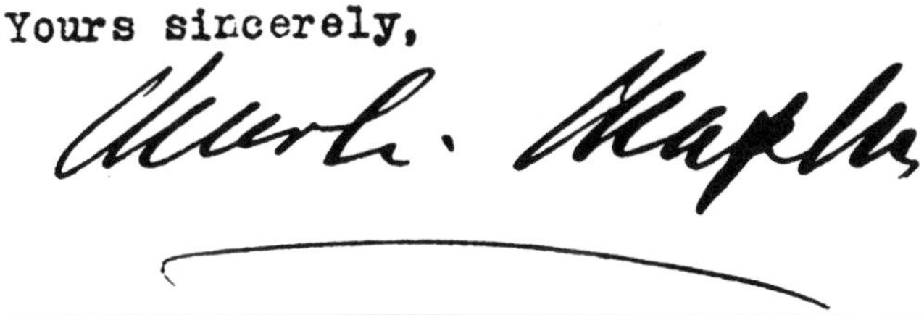

Yours sincerely,

Charlie Chaplin, **$100.**

Gary Cooper, **$125.**

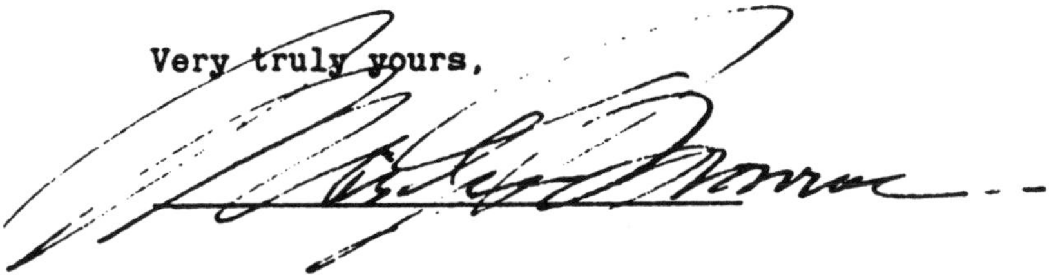

Very truly yours,

Marilyn Monroe, **$350.**

Bud Abbott and Lou Costello, **$125.**

Clark Gable, **$150.**

Rudolf Valentino, **$600.**

Carole Landis, **$35.**

Lon Chaney, **$1,000.**

Cecil B. DeMille, **$75.**

Katharine Hepburn, **$10.**

Edward G. Robinson, **$25.**

There are now more collectors of movie star autographs in the hobby than there are of any other specific category. Accordingly, the autographs of the major film stars have increased dramatically in price over the past few years. However, movie star autographs can be the trickiest to collect of all the possible categories, since virtually every kind of fake, fraud, or forgery exists within the realm of movie material. There are signatures by rubber stamps, autopens (John Wayne used one, for example), secretaries, fan mail services, and forgers. Some fan photographs were printed with signatures on the negative of the photograph (printed facsimiles), and the movie studios in the 1930s and 1940s answered almost all autograph requests with secretarial signatures. Be aware that these problems are not insurmountable; you should, after some practice, be able to authenticate most of your movie star collection. However, you should realize some of the problems inherent in the movie field before you buy or sell these autographs or become too deeply involved with them.

There are several ways to approach the collecting of movie material, and several ways to specialize in various sub-categories. Someday, many movie autographs will be collected as historical autographs (as classical stage actors and actresses are now regarded by some collectors). Some movie star collectors are intent upon capturing the history of Hollywood by way of letters and signed photographs of the early movie moguls and directors like D.W. Griffith. Early movie stars, especially those involved in Hollywood scandals, such as "Fatty" Arbuckle, Mary Miles Minter, Olive Thomas, and Wallace Reid are very much in demand. These autographs are among the most expensive in the movie category, with signed photographs of Griffith, Arbuckle, and Reid selling for upwards of $200 each. There are quite a few letters and documents regarding the early cinema, and many of these, even if not signed by anyone especially famous, have sold for high prices.

Collectors are attracted to motion picture autographs by their beauty and variety. Signed movie scenes, lobby cards, or pinups of popular actors and actresses make excellent and attractive display pieces, and they are great fun to collect. Collectors have specialized by collecting the signed photographs of Academy Award winners, pinup stars, western stars, or signed scenes from famous films. The signed still photographs are especially good ways to collect movie autographs, because even if a star is not extremely well-known, their film may be. The most popular signed stills have included scenes from *Tarzan*, *The Public Enemy* (the classic "grapefruit" scene with James Cagney and Mae Clarke), *Singin' in the Rain, Gone with the Wind,* and various "Frankenstein" films. Collecting signed movie stills may lead to collecting "double-signed" photographs by more than one star of a film. These can be collected rather easily by mail or through dealers. Sometimes requests by mail can be risky. One collector sent a signed scene from the 1934 film, *Cleopatra,* already signed by the star, Claudette Colbert, to the late actor Henry Wilcoxon for his signature. Wilcoxon liked the photograph so much that he decided to keep it and send another in its place. A general rule for collecting double-signed photographs is to always send to the lesser star first. A major star is more likely to sign a photograph if it is already signed by another person. They are less tempted to keep photos signed by minor stars.

Since photographs are the most widely sought after form for movie autographs, some controversy has arisen in the hobby over whether it is best to have a photograph that is inscribed, i.e., signed "To Joe, Marilyn Monroe," or uninscribed. There are a number of arguments on both sides of the issue, but, as far as value is concerned, a photograph is more valuable if uninscribed, unless you count the sentimental value of owning one inscribed to you. Exceptions to this are very rare photographs where you are lucky to find the autograph in any form.

Aside from signed photographs, signatures on album leaves, index cards, books, scripts, lobby cards, and movie posters are also widely collected. Oftentimes these make more interesting items than signed photographs. Simple signatures on cards or album pages may not be as glamorous as photographs or posters, but they are more versatile since they can be framed and matted with photographs of your choice.

As we have mentioned, the presence of many unauthentic movie star autographs makes collecting in this field a bit more difficult. Most unauthentic movie signatures are those signed by secretaries. When the Hollywood studio system began, studios were inundated with fan mail for the various actors and actresses. Rather than turn this mail over to the stars to handle, the studios employed dozens of secretaries to forge stars' signatures on letters, photographs, and other memorabilia. In an interview with a collector, the silent screen actress Colleen Moore stated that when she was a star, she never signed autograph requests that came through the mail. This was also true of every other major and minor star as well. From around 1925 to 1955, stars never signed through the mail except for professional contacts or for very special friends. The only "vintage" movie autographs that are likely to be authentic are those that were signed in person. Never purchase vintage material unless the seller provides proof of authenticity, evidence that the signature was obtained in person, or has material for sale such as a check or contract that the star legally had to sign.

With the demise of the studio system in the 1950s, it became the responsibility of the star to handle his or her own fan mail. Many of the older stars began to sign for fans through the mail, and today more than 95 percent of the older stars personally autograph and answer their fan mail. You are a very special person to them. Nevertheless, there are a few older stars, and many younger stars, who employ secretaries or fan mail services to answer autograph requests. The following is an incomplete list of past and present stars who delegate others to sign most of their autograph requests, or who did so before their deaths: John Belushi, Charles Bronson, Richard Burton, Dick Clark, Jackie Coogan, Angie Dickinson, Richard Dreyfuss, Howard Duff, Jimmy Durante, Alice Faye, James Garner, Greer Garson, Bonita Granville, Bob Hope, Shirley MacLaine, Fred MacMurray, Mary Tyler Moore, Liza Minnelli, Paul Newman, Lloyd Nolan, Sidney Poitier, Burt Reynolds, Randolph Scott, Brooke Shields, Sylvester Stallone, Elizabeth Taylor, Robert Wagner, Raquel Welch, and Natalie Wood. This is not to say that every signature received through the mail from these individuals is bad; on the contrary, a good letter such as the type we advocate will often elicit a genuine example. The unauthentic signatures are not difficult to spot because many secretaries and fan mail services just aren't that good. We will discuss authenticating your collection in the next chapter.

Daryl Hannah.

Diane Keaton.

John Travolta.

Bill Murray.

Values range from $5 to $10 each.

87

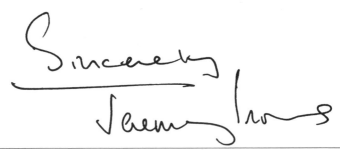

Jeremy Irons.

Matthew Broderick.

Michelle Pfeiffer.

Kelly LeBrock.

Brooke Shields.

Joan Collins.

Pictured examples, **$5 to $10 each.**

88

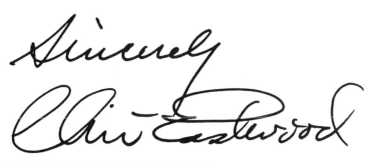

Clint Eastwood.

Sally Field.

Larry Hagman.

Bo Derek.

Julie Walters.

Values range from **$5 to $10 each.**

89

Hundreds of stars of the past and present almost always answer autograph requests with authentic signatures if you write to them at their home addresses. A small sample of these stars include Fred Astaire, Katharine Hepburn, Robert Young, Shirley Temple, and Meryl Streep.

If you are patient with your collection of movie star autographs and receptive to new information that might help you authenticate your collection, you should be able to build a valuable collection in the coming years. Currently, signatures of stars who willingly sign can be sold from $3 to $5 each, with signed photographs selling for $8 to $15. Signatures of recently deceased or rarer stars usually sell in the $5 to $15 range, with signed photographs going for $10 to $25, depending on the star's fame and the scarcity of the autograph.

Besides the explosion in collecting the autographs of movie stars in recent years, there has been a similar growth in the number of sports related collectors. All aspects of sports collecting, including the collection of baseball cards, programs, and player uniforms, have been on the increase throughout the 1970s and 1980s, and autographs have been no exception. The signatures of the majority of current athletes in baseball, football, basketball, hockey, and boxing are worth about $1 each, but superstar's signatures can sell for $3 to $5 each, with signed photographs priced at $8 to $15 depending on the fame of the athlete and the scarcity of the signature. Even more worthy of collecting than the modern personalities are the sports legends or Hall of Fame members from each sport. Living Hall of Fame members in baseball, football, or basketball are not difficult to obtain through the mail, especially since the respective Hall of Fame offices will forward your letters to the players. Home addresses are also readily available, and there are several address books that list virtually every living member of each major sport.

Most sports players also do their own autographing, so secretarial and other spurious signatures are less common than with movie stars, for example. Some players have used secretaries and others to sign autographs for them. These include Hank Aaron, Willie Mays, Sandy Koufax, Ted Williams, and Joe DiMaggio (who had his sister sign for him for many years). A few players (Mickey Mantle and Reggie Jackson) have even gone to such extremes as to have batboys sign their fan mail and autograph balls for distribution at the stadiums.

Secretarial sports signatures are most commonly received through writing to the player in care of his team's stadium. Occasionally, someone in the front office will do the signing rather than the player himself. Autopen signatures are almost non-existent in sports (golfer Jack Nicklaus is the only one I know of) but rubber stamps are fairly common and are used by Willie McCovey, Mickey Mantle, Ted Williams, and golfer Ben Hogan. Since rubber stamps do not confuse many people, they are not much of a problem. Overall, sports signatures are usually good bets to be authentic. There is certainly a lot less forgery in sports than in almost any other field.

James "Cool Papa" Bell.

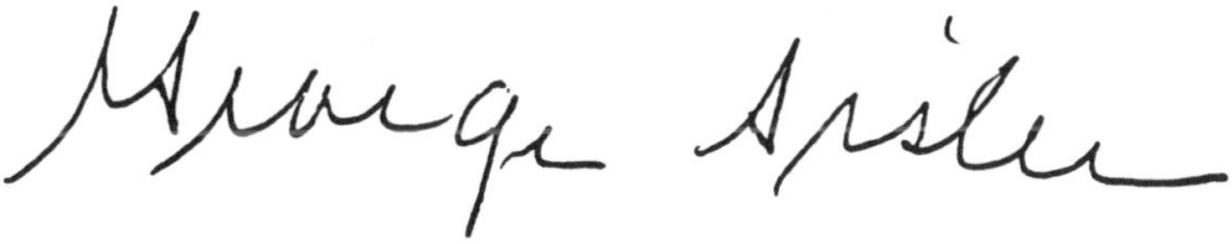

George Sisler.

Babe Ruth, **$175.**

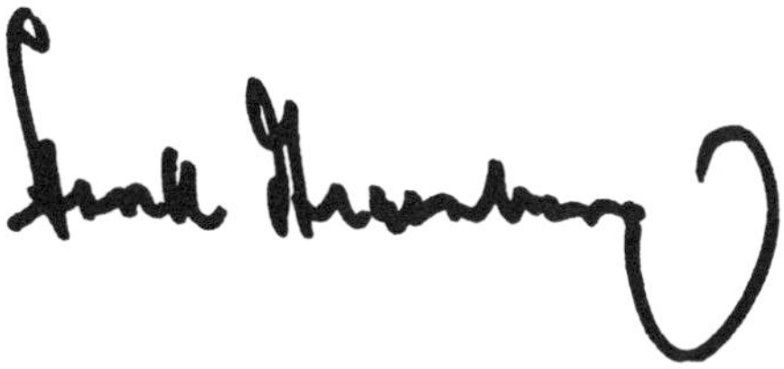

Warren Spahn.

Hank Greenberg.

Yogi Berra.

Carl Hubbell.

Hank Aaron.

Gabby Hartnett.

Stan Musial.

Max Carey.

Values $5 to $15 each unless noted.

Bob Feller.

91

Zack Wheat.

Rube Marquard.

Goose Goslin.

Sandy Koufax.

Frank Frisch.

Lefty Grove.

Dizzy Dean.

Values $5 to $15 each unless noted.

Glenn Wright, **$10.**

Signed photograph of baseball's only one-armed player, Pete Gray, **$25.**

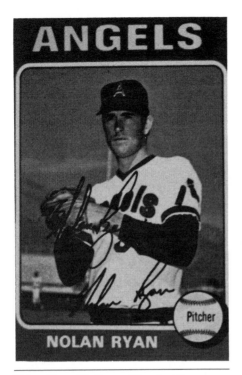

Ted Williams (© T.C.M.A., Ltd.), **$5.**

Nolan Ryan (© Topps Chewing Gum,
Inc.), **$5.**

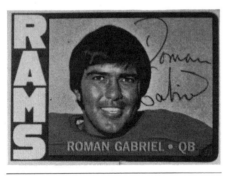

Roman Gabriel (© Topps Chewing Gum,
Inc.), **$5.**

Bob Feller (© T.C.M.A., Ltd.), **$5.**

Within sports autographs, there is also a very wide range of auxiliary material to be collected. Besides file cards, photographs or letters, sports autographs are often found on baseballs, footballs, uniforms, baseball cards, and special types of postcards, like the Hall of Fame plaque reproduction postcards issued by the Baseball Hall of Fame. Imagination in collecting sports autographs can really pay off because some sports memorabilia (baseball cards or uniforms) is very valuable even when unsigned. If you collect baseball or other cards and are able to get them autographed, you will greatly enhance the value of already valuable material.

Baseball autographs are the most widely collected sports autographs, followed by boxing, football, and the Olympics. The autographs from hockey, basketball, and soccer stars are also collected, but to a smaller degree. Autographs of golf and tennis stars are in great demand and carry moderate to high price tags. The big names in almost all areas of sports are worthwhile autographs to collect, but you might also be interested in collecting "record breakers" from various sports, or "sports oddities" such as the autograph of Eddie Gaedel, the only midget to play major league baseball. Some collectors are intent upon collecting nearly every person who has played a particular sport, living or deceased, and you can certainly attempt this feat if you wish. There are address books for sports stars listing almost every living player of a particular sport. Sports oriented publications like *The Autograph Review* publish advertisements by dealers selling signatures of hundreds of obscure deceased players.

Yet, unless you are collecting for enjoyment only, it is best to stick to the Babe Ruths, Otto Grahams, and Muhammad Alis. There are excellent investments to be made with the top people in the sports realm, especially with the autographs of legends such as Babe Ruth and Red Grange, and with team-signed baseballs, footballs, or basketballs. Sports collecting can be one of the most enjoyable and profitable autograph fields if you use your imagination to make it so.

If you want to be even more sure that the autographs you collect are genuine, try collecting original cartoon art or the signatures of cartoonists. Although it is always possible to receive a cartoon sketch of a character through the mail that has been drawn and signed by the cartoonist's assistant, this seldom occurs except with very famous animators such as Walt Disney. Most signed cartoon sketches are the work of the cartoonist himself, and they are fairly easy to obtain.

Original signed cartoon art is obtained through the mail by writing to the cartoonist in care of his or her syndicator. Most cartoonists will draw their characters for you on a file card if you ask them politely. Two important exceptions are Jim Davis (Garfield) and Charles Schulz (Peanuts) who rarely send sketches or even their signatures. Cartoon art, obtained through the mail for roughly fifty cents, can be sold immediately for anywhere from $5 to $25, depending upon the character, the cartoonist, the scarcity of the item, and the elaboration of the sketch (a full-length portrait of the character or just the head or face of the character).

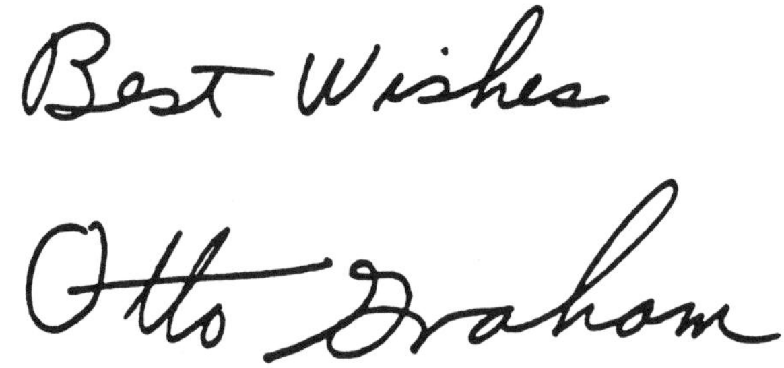

Best Wishes

Otto Graham

Otto Graham.

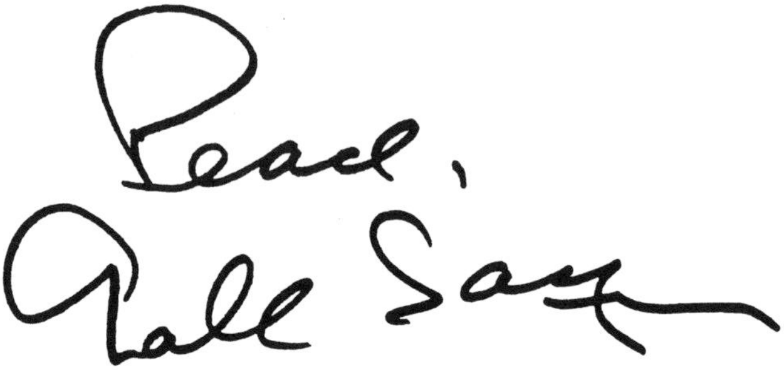

Peace,
Gale Sayers

Gale Sayers.

Johnny Unitas

Johnny Unitas.

Bart Starr

Bart Starr.

Bronko Nagurski

Bronko Nagurski.

Values, $5 to $10 each.

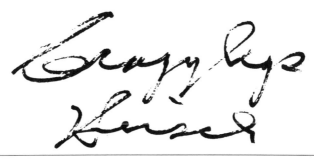

Crazy Legs Hirsch.

Dick Butkus.

"Red" Grange.

Sid Luckman.

Sam Baugh.

Values, **$5 to $10 each.**

Glenn Davis signature

Glenn Davis.

My best wishes to you, Bob – Kyle Rote

Kyle Rote.

Boxing great Floyd Patterson, **$15.**

There are two collectible groups of cartoon sketches: those from the creators or artists involved in animated cartoons, or those from newspaper or magazine cartoonists. It is more difficult to obtain original, signed sketches from animators, but these are usually more valuable and worthwhile. A signed sketch of a Disney character by Walt Disney would be worth a fortune if one could be located. The problem is that Disney never actually created his characters and seldom if ever drew them. Mickey Mouse was actually created by animator Ub Iwerks. Like most early animators, including Max Fleischer, Pat Sullivan (Felix the Cat), and Walter Lantz, Disney served mostly as a studio boss rather than a cartoonist. Although "Disney" autographs were sent out by the studio, these were actually signed by studio animators such as Floyd Gottfredson, Hank Porter, and Bob Moore. Even the famous

Animator Walter Lantz, **$15.** (© Walter Lantz Productions.)

Animator Bob Clampett with some of his cartoon characters, **$15.**

Disney signature shown at the beginning of the television program, "The Wonderful World of Disney" bears little resemblance to Disney's actual signature, which is worth approximately $125.

Nevertheless, signed sketches of Disney characters by Disney artists and animators can be worth a great deal of money. A signed original panel of a 1930s strip cartoon by Floyd Gottfredson (signing Disney's name) recently sold for $1,500. It is possible to obtain by mail sketches of Disney characters by animators and cartoonists such as Eldon Dedini, Ward Kimball, Hank Ketcham, and Carl Barks, all of whom worked for Disney. And there are many other characters you can obtain, by mail or from dealers, signed by animators such as Chuck Jones (Bugs Bunny and other Warner Brothers characters); Walter Lantz (Woody Woodpecker); Otto Messmer (the true creator of Felix the Cat); or Max Fleischer (Betty Boop). In addition, signatures of the great animators of the past such as Fleischer, Messmer, Tex Avery, and others, can be purchased and possibly framed with photographs or prints of the cartoon characters.

Exciting, original pieces of artwork can be obtained from newspaper and magazine cartoonists. Many dealers also sell original artwork and signed original daily panels of both living and deceased cartoonists. Signatures of Rube Goldberg, Harold Gray, Ham Fisher, Otto Soglow, Chic Young, Al Capp, and Roy Crane, all deceased, are readily available. Some of the best bets for investment purposes include newspaper cartoonists Garry Trudeau (Doonesbury), who rarely sketches for collectors; Hank Ketcham (Dennis the Menace); Charles Schulz; Jim Davis; Johnny Hart (B.C.); Reg Smythe (Andy Capp); and Bud Sagendorf (Popeye). Magazine cartoonists are often less famous than the "strip" cartoonists, but are also worth collecting. Some of the best in this category include Charles Addams, Sam Gross, Chon Day, and Gahan Wilson. Political cartoonists are very popular and will often sketch some of the nation's political leaders for you. The most popular political cartoonists include Pat Oliphant, Tony Auth, Herbert Block, Jeff MacNelly (who also draws the strip character, Shoe), and John Trever. Political cartoonists can be addressed in care of their syndicators. Write to magazine cartoonists in care of the magazine in which their cartoon appears. Home addresses are also available for many cartoonists.

Sincerely

Max Fleischer

1932

Max Fleischer, **$35.**

Best wishes

MILTON CANIFF

2 April 1981

Milton Caniff.

HIRSCHFELD

6/30/81

Al Hirschfeld.

JOHN CULLEN MURPHY

John Cullen Murphy.

Charles Addams.

Jules Feiffer.

9/19/80

Chester Gould.

Charles Schulz.

102 Values, **$5 to $10 each** unless noted.

Joe Palooka & HAM FISHER.

Ham Fisher, **$25.**

Norman Maurer of The Three Stooges, **$5.**

Everett Raymond Kinstler (Zorro), **$15.**

Felix the Cat by Otto Messmer (© King Features Syndicate), **$75.**

Thomas Cheney, **$5.**

Edwina Dumm (Tippie), **$10.**

There are three main advantages to collecting cartoon art. First of all, it is easy to obtain. Second, except in the case of Walt Disney, secretarial or forged material is rare. And finally, these items make wonderful display pieces. Even when the cartoonist is relatively unknown, the character is almost always recognizable, and that fact gives value to the item.

The autographs of many of the current stars of popular or rock music such as Bruce Springsteen, Michael Jackson, Prince, and Madonna can be sold for fairly high prices immediately, if you are lucky enough to obtain such material. There is a tremendous demand for all the latest superstars of popular music, and a very low supply of their autographs. Rock and roll musicians are probably the toughest to obtain of all modern autographs short of current presidents. Because rock personalities are nearly always on tour, or without permanent addresses, it is nearly impossible to reach them by mail. Tight concert security also makes it difficult to get their autographs in person.

Items signed by rock personalities can be very interesting and attractive, especially in the form of signed record albums, concert posters or programs, or even signed musical quotations or song lyrics. The main problem with collecting rock stars, however, is that many of today's stars will lose their popularity. In ten to fifteen years the values of their autographs could decrease. Exceptions to this rule are the musicians of the 1950s, 1960s, and 1970s whose popularity has remained fairly constant over the years. Included in this category are people like Buddy Holly, Chuck Berry, Elvis Presley, the Beatles, Bob Dylan, the Rolling Stones, The Who, Jimi Hendrix, Janis Joplin, and Jim Morrison ("The Doors"). All of these are also difficult to obtain, and can sometimes command exorbitant prices. Secretarial and forged examples are relatively rare and mostly emanate from record companies. Several secretarial examples of the Beatles' signatures were obtained in the 1960s from record labels.

Country, jazz, folk, blues, and soul music are also part of the popular music field, but these autographs are much easier to obtain, even through the mail, since home addresses are readily available.

If you are intent upon collecting in this field, there are a few things you can do to build your collection. Since rock star home addresses are rare, you might try writing to the musician in care of the concert stadium where they might be appearing for one or more days. (Concert schedules are printed in *Rolling Stone* and other magazines.) This has to be timed correctly to get your letter to the star on the correct dates (ask the Post Office for help). It is best to send photographs or other memorabilia, because large packages are more likely to attract the attention of the performer and the stadium officials. I know that this is hard to believe, but this approach actually works more often than not. Since rock autographs are also hard to obtain in person at large stadiums, try attending smaller shows by rock, country, jazz and blues musicians at clubs in and around your area. You won't find the biggest names this way, but club owners are usually very helpful in getting autographs for you, or allowing you backstage to get them yourself. You probably can obtain the autographs of quite a few older performers or even future stars in this manner. By following these

The Beatles (John Lennon, Paul McCartney, George Harrison, Ringo Starr, **$550.**

Jim Morrison, **$75.**

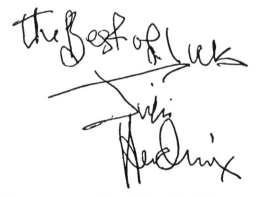

Jimi Hendrix, **$200.**

Muddy Waters (signature)

Muddy Waters, **$15.**

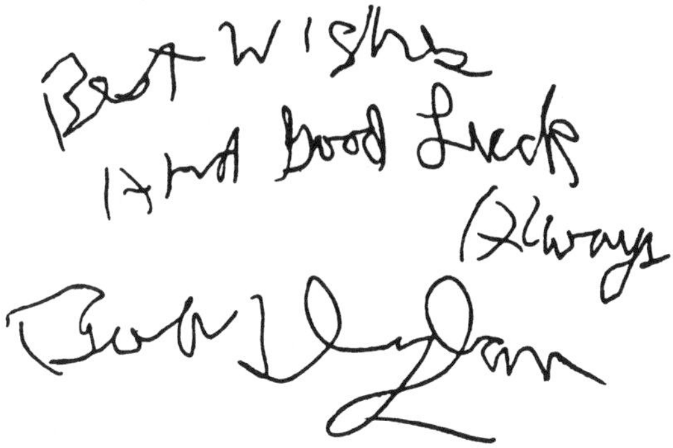

Best Wishes And Good Luck Always (signature) *Bob Dylan*

Bob Dylan, **$20.**

Linda Ronstadt (signature)

Linda Ronstadt, **$5.**

Much love, *Stevie Nicks* (signature)

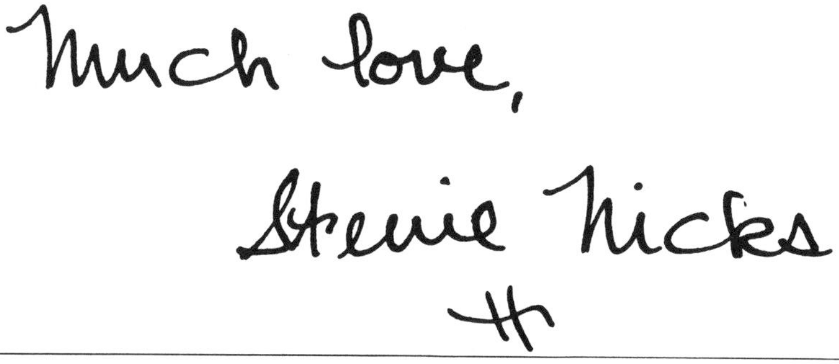

Stevie Nicks, **$5.**

Little Richard (signature)

Little Richard, **$10.**

Peter, Paul, and Mary (Peter Yarrow, Paul Stookey, Mary Travers), **$25.**

B. B. King, **$5.**

Neil Young, **$15.**

Bob Dylan, **$50.**

Eric Clapton, **$35.**

Jerry Garcia of The Grateful Dead (photograph by Robert A. Minkin), **$30.**

Album signed in person by Gregg Allman of The Allman Brothers, **$40.**

suggestions, you should be able to acquire most of the rock and popular music autographs you desire with some time and perseverance.

Popular autographs are fun to collect, make excellent items for display, and can be good investment material.

If you are cautious about secretarials and other unauthentic autographs, and choose the type of material you collect with care, you can build a collection of popular cultural material that is both interesting and potentially very valuable.

8

Authenticating Your Collection

As we have suggested throughout this book, the biggest problem you'll experience when collecting autographs is determining which autographs are authentic. One of the joys of autograph collecting is the waiting by the mailbox each day hoping to find it stuffed with autographs. But nothing spoils this joy more than the discovery that the autograph you've just received (or worse yet, purchased from an inexperienced seller) is not authentic. Unauthentic autographs are, of course, valueless. Although it sometimes takes a lot of hard work to uncover unauthentic autographs, you'll probably be able to verify almost every signature in your collection after some practice. Furthermore, to survive in the autograph field, you're going to need to learn how to authenticate your autographs whether you are buying, selling, or only collecting through the mail.

The easiest unauthentic signatures to detect are printed facsimiles. These often appear on photographs sent out by baseball stadiums or movie studios, or on White House cards that bear facsimile signatures of the president. Printed facsimiles are either signatures produced on a printing press or are signatures made on the negative of a photograph before it is reproduced. They are easy to detect because it is not hard to tell the difference between printer's ink and pen ink. Pen ink is shiny, shaded, has no breaks in the script, and varies in the color and weight of the strokes. Printer's ink is dull, lacks color variations or weight variations, and features minute breaks in the script.

Since all of the signatures in this book are printed facsimiles, you should have no trouble comparing them to real handwriting. Sign your name in black felt pen on a piece of paper and compare it to the signatures printed in the book. You'll be able to see immediately some of the differences. Although some ink, such as old india ink, has no real feel to it, you might try feeling the surface of your signed card or photographs lightly to detect the presence of ink or indentations made by a pen. But be careful.

Some of the movie star printed facsimiles in circulation are machine stamped onto the photograph, giving them the appearance of being actually signed. This is because the writing is indented into the photograph, albeit in a uniform manner. No real person can indent as uniformly as a machine, and this is your clue. If you aren't able to detect a printed facsimile on your own at first, take the items to a printer or photographer. They can easily identify the ink for you or let you know whether a signature is part of the photograph or has been added by a pen. Printed facsimiles should prove no problem to you. Usually, they don't succeed in fooling even non-collectors who receive them from baseball or movie stars in response to fan letters.

Rubber stamps, commonly used by sports players and a few movie stars such as Carol Burnett, Robert Redford, and Michael Caine, are also fairly easy to detect, depending on how well the stamp was made and the type of ink that was used. Stamps using an ordinary ink pad seldom fool anyone, but long ago, when india ink was used (mostly by silent movie stars such as Theda Bara and Ruth Roland), stamps turned out very convincing signatures. Virtually the only way to uncover these frauds today is to compare them with another copy in the same way autopen signatures are detected. Modern rubber stamps show no color variations in the ink and no weight variations unless the stamp was poorly applied. In that case, no one is fooled by it. They often leave other ink marks

Robert Redford's rubber-stamped signature on photographs, no value.

unless the stamp was perfectly applied. Rubber stamps look especially poor on a glossy photograph since they often slip in the application and leave smudges. On paper or a card, the ink tends to soak into the paper more than ink would if actually signed by a person. Try to remember that the human hand, unlike a rubber stamp, produces a signature with weight and speed variations, and this leads to color variations and differences in the thickness of the pen strokes. Rubber stamps cannot duplicate these human characteristics. The only area to exercise caution regarding possible rubber-stamped signatures is with old, dark, matt-finished photographs with the "signatures" in india ink. All others pose no real problems.

Very-hard-to-identify rubber stamp signature, that of silent actress Theda Bara, who used a stamp to answer most of her requests for autographs.

THE WHITE HOUSE

WASHINGTON

August 3, 1979

To Mr. and Mrs. Frank Miglis

Rosalynn and I take great pleasure in congratulating you on your 60th wedding anniversary. We hope that you will enjoy special happiness on this day and throughout the year ahead.

Sincerely,

Jimmy Carter

Mr. and Mrs. Frank Miglis
Maplewood Park
Center Rutland, Vermont   05736

Jimmy Carter L.S., with autopen.

Autopen signatures receive a lot of attention in some autograph publications and are seen as threats to the hobby by many collectors and dealers. Although the autopen poses a threat in that it prevents the average person or amateur collector from obtaining the genuine signatures of presidents, astronauts, or military leaders, the machine has failed to deceive the experienced collector or dealer. To detect the use of an autopen, remember that two signatures made from the same "pattern" (a copy of the person's signature placed into the machine) can be superimposed upon one another exactly. Pattern wear can cause them to look slightly different, but not enough to fool the educated eye. Autopen signatures do not look like they were actually signed by human beings in any case. Like the rubber stamp, there are no speed or weight variations within the signature, and, because they are written more slowly than the average person writes, the ink sometimes soaks into the

Ronald Reagan (two patterns).

John Young.

Billy Joel.

George Bush.

William H. Rehnquist.

Kurt Waldheim.

Omar N. Bradley.

Helmut Schmidt.

Examples of autopen patterns

Jack Nicklaus.

Jerry Ford.

Richard Nixon.

Jeremiah Denton.

Examples of autopen patterns

paper. These clues alone do not necessarily prove that the signature was made by autopen, but they are pretty good indications. The only sure method is to compare your signature with a known autopen pattern. These are published in all of the autograph publications, and the editors make a great effort to track down every pattern used by every major person. For example, Presidents Nixon and Ford have used over ten patterns each, and many other famous names have one or more patterns, usually for the various forms of their signature. As mentioned earlier, sending more than one item for

signature makes hunting for patterns unnecessary, because the signatures can be tested as soon as they are out of the envelope.

If you come across a handwritten letter or inscribed photograph, do not assume that it isn't an autopen. There are new autopens capable of generating "handwritten" inscriptions or letters of some length. It is also possible for a secretary to add a handwritten inscription above an autopen signature. Don't let this worry you, though. If you keep an eye out for autopen patterns, and treat carefully

Model Christie Brinkley used an autopen to sign this photograph in the upper left-hand corner and added a handwritten inscription. When the picture was returned to her, she had a secretary sign it in the lower right portion.

the material you receive from presidents, astronauts, and military personnel, you should have no problem with the autopen. This is just one more challenge, and most collectors handle it with ease.

The signatures that do pose a major problem for collectors are secretarial and forged signatures. Secretarial signatures are signed either by the celebrity's personal assistant or an agency or firm that specializes in answering fan mail or signing autographs. In both cases, they are forged signatures. However, we have a technical nicety here. One is "legally" forged (authorized by the celebrity); the unauthorized signature is illegal. Do not sign Ronald Reagan's name on a piece of paper and

try to sell it or otherwise pass it off as authentic. You would be guilty of forgery. Illegal forgeries appear both on modern and historical material.

The first thing that you must do to eliminate secretarials or forged signatures is to obtain facsimiles of the person's authentic signature, such as the authentic signatures printed throughout this book. Examples are readily available from almost any celebrity of the past or present. The major source for film and popular music signatures is Roger Christensen's *The Ultimate Movie, TV, and Rock Directory (1984)*. Sources for most other signatures are the many books of Charles Hamilton such as *The Signature of America* (1979), and the two-volume *American Autographs,* (1983). These books are listed in the Bibliography, and the Hamilton books, which are fairly expensive, can be found in the reference section of larger libraries. You can also use items such as checks or contracts legally signed by the celebrity to authenticate your material if you can find these from other collectors or autograph dealers.

Once you have found true facsimiles of the individuals whose autographs you wish to authenticate, you must keep in mind one very important rule regarding facsimiles before you begin to use them. Don't take them too seriously. Some facsimiles, such as many of those printed in Roger Christensen's book, are of autographs obtained in person, and thus are usually signed more awkwardly and hurriedly. These will be helpful to you, but don't assume that your signature is not authentic because it is not scribbled as fast as the in-person signature.

RONALD REAGAN
August 10, 1979

Mr. & Mrs. Frank Miglis
c/o Bob Bennett
One Governor's Lane
Shelburne, VT 05482

Dear Mr. & Mrs. Miglis:

I want to join with your family and friends in wishing you a very Happy 60th Wedding Anniversary.

What a special day this is for you. I know it will be one filled with wonderful memories.

Nancy joins me in sending our best.

Sincerely,

Ronald Reagan

RONALD REAGAN

10960 WILSHIRE BOULEVARD, LOS ANGELES, CALIFORNIA 90024

Ronald Reagan's secretary signed this letter for him. Compare the signature to the one in chapter 5.

Authentic

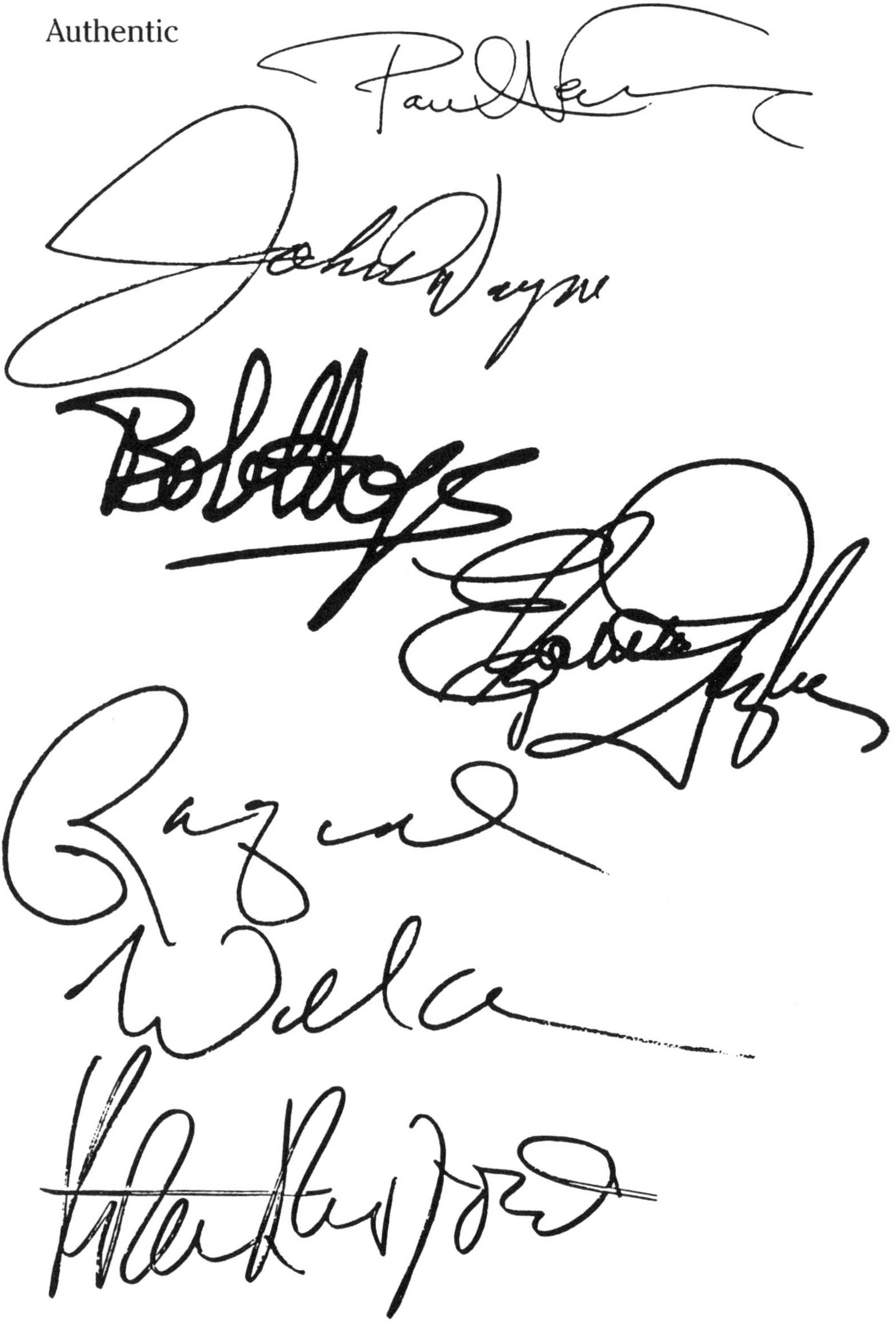

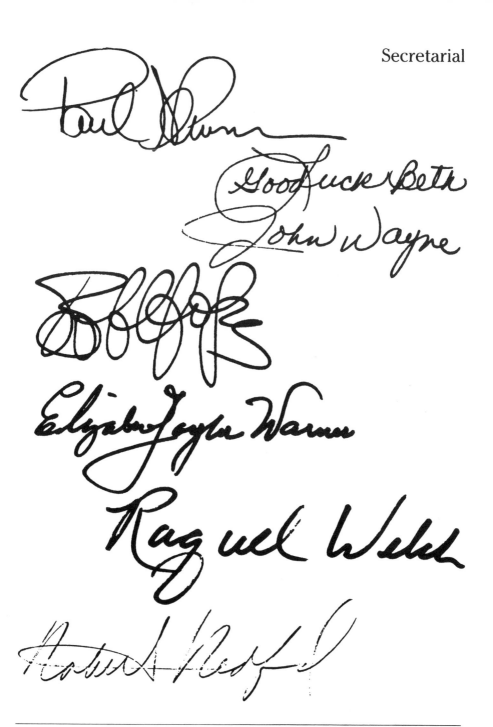

Authentic signatures of Raquel Welch, Bob Hope, Paul Newman, Robert Redford, John Wayne, and Elizabeth Taylor are pictured at left.

Other signatures may have been signed by a person at a different period in life than your signature, which may affect how it appears to you, or it may have been signed while the person was ill. The point to remember is that you should not treat any one facsimile as the "bible" on a certain personality. Instead, look for general characteristics in the signature that will help you to spot a trend in the celebrity's writing style.

Keeping the main rule in mind, here are the five factors to assist you in comparing your signatures.

1 Remember, most secretarials are not that good. Secretaries, and those who forge autographs may occasionally fool even experienced collectors, but they are seldom so skilled as to avoid discovery. A person's actual signature varies at least slightly every single time. A very good secretary or forger may pick up on some of these variations, but never all of them. In most cases, the secretarial or forged signature is copied from one "master" signature from the celebrity, not 1,001 variations. A secretary may reproduce some visible characteristics but will not be able to give it the total style of the celebrity. Some secretaries will write slowly and be too attentive to detail in a signature, in which case the slowness of the signature will give it away, or the secretary may write too fast, with little or no detail, which is a pretty good indicator to the trained eye. Speed comparison is probably the most important giveaway.

2 Try to find an authentic signature of a celebrity that was not signed in person. Compare it to your signature. You should be able to match the relative speeds between the two signatures and be able to see if there is any detail lacking in your signature. This should help you to determine the authenticity of the item.

3 Watch for angles and letter formation. In authenticating material, look for similarities or differences in the angles of the two signatures you are comparing. A person will usually keep the same angular relationships constant throughout their handwriting. A secretary may not pick up on details as insignificant as these appear to be. In addition, a celebrity will usually form letters in the same way, something a secretary may not be able to duplicate exactly. The little things are often the things that give the secretary or forger away!

4 Note the size and position of the signature. Try to find facsimiles that have not been reduced in size. There are many publications that publish them full-sized. A celebrity tends to write his or her signature the same size if the material being signed (photograph, file card, etc.) is the same. In addition, signatures on lined file cards are easier to authenticate than other signatures. Why? Because, with lines, the size and position of two signatures can be measured more easily. However, without a lined card, you can still compare the general sizes and positions of the signatures, even on different materials.

5 The "feel" test. Glance over the two signatures you are comparing and look for some common characteristics of the two. Look for small and shaky handwriting, slowness, mistakes or evidences of erasure, inaccuracies, and how the ink soaks into the paper. Try to get a "feel" of the writing in the two signatures. If it doesn't seem right to you, there is a good chance that your signature is not authentic.

Authentication will be difficult for you at first. Make no mistake, it is not easy work. But if you are patient with your comparisons, you should have no trouble after awhile with either secretarial or forged signatures. Until you feel secure with your decisions, try sending copies of your signatures to autograph dealers with a self-addressed, stamped envelope, and ask for their opinion. Most will be glad to help you. There are also autograph magazines, such as *Newsreel* that publishes an annual facsimile issue showing both common secretarial and authentic signatures of many celebrities, and these sources might be of assistance to you.

While you are still inexperienced at authentication, you must take pains to avoid purchasing autographs that are not genuine. First of all, you should buy only from reputable dealers who are, at the least, members of the UACC or The Manuscript Society. Secondly, buy only from dealers who carry a money-back guarantee of authenticity in their catalogs. If you purchase anything from a dealer that you feel uncomfortable about, photocopy the item and sent it to another dealer for an opinion. (Do not, however, tell them that it was purchased from a competitor.)

Forgeries by sellers of autographs are not uncommon. In the past three or four years it was proved that a West Coast art student and an East Coast autograph firm both forged movie star autographs on photographs. In both cases, very rare signed photographs, such as Greta Garbo's and Katharine Hepburn's (who almost never signs photographs, except for her personal friends), were offered, and, in the case of Hepburn, in unlimited quantities. As we mentioned when discussing historical forgeries, beware of deals that are too good to be true. They usually are. Always buy from experienced autograph dealers until you think that you have learned enough about authenticating autographs to do it yourself.

As with writing to celebrities through the mail for their autographs, you need patience when you are attempting to authenticate your collection. Proceed slowly at first, and you will gradually find it much easier. Don't be afraid to write to the dealers listed in this book for assistance. If your request is polite and courteous, and you enclose a self-addressed, stamped envelope, they will help you. Many people are leery of authenticating their collection because they believe that they simply won't be able to do it correctly. Don't be afraid of this, either. Authentication is difficult, but certainly not impossible.

9

Preserving Your Collection

As your autograph collection grows in size and value, you must learn to protect it from heat, light, and moisture damage. It is also advisable to keep a current record of your collection for insurance purposes. This is to protect yourself from the financial loss a fire or other disaster might cause. The value of your autographs will appreciate if you learn to frame and mat them attractively or have this done by a professional. In this chapter we will explain how to secure, preserve, and increase the value of your collection.

Once you have obtained a signed photograph, letter, or signature, you must store it where is will be protected from tears or creasing and not exposed to extreme light, heat, or moisture. There are several ways to do this, but some are better than others. The best method to protect your autographs is to place them in a three-ring binder, between acetate sheets. These acetate sheets will protect your items from too much handling as well as from moisture and dust. Some collectors buy photograph albums containing plastic sheets with sticky surfaces in which they place their autographs. Although the surface of the sheets may not seem to be too sticky to you, if these albums are stacked on top of one another, or, if the photographs or letters are not removed after a period of months, it becomes very difficult to remove them without risk of tearing them. You can remedy this problem by placing sheets of paper on top of the sticky surface if you wish, but acetate sheets are still better because they don't fully enclose the item and they provide a flexible backing. Plastic sheets can also be used in a three-ring binder, but if you decide to use them, make sure to back the photo with a piece of cardboard. The plastic is usually too flexible to protect your photographs from bending. I do not recommend storing your autographs in file boxes or folders. Although these are inexpensive methods of storage, the photographs or letters can move around easily and often become scratched or otherwise damaged, with the constant contact of other material.

Extreme dryness can cause photographs or old paper to crack, and moisture is also very detrimental to your autographs. Moisture can cause stains in the paper, or make the ink "bleed," smear, or become distorted. After many years, it can cause the items to become moldy, or otherwise ruin them. To protect your items from moisture, store them at room temperature, but not in the attic or the basement. If your house is too moist, you may want to purchase a dehumidifier to protect your valuable collection, or avoid the problem by storing your autograph albums in desk drawers or cabinets.

Light is another threat, because direct light can fade signatures or signed photographs, and that just about ruins them. Avoid framing your autographs and hanging them on the walls of your house, especially if there is a great deal of sunlight streaming into the room. Electric light, if bright enough, can also be just as harmful. If you must display your autographs on the wall, make sure that they are in a softly lighted room, with little or no sunlight coming in. The best place would probably be a recreation room in which temperature and moisture were maintained at normal levels.

Besides storing your autographs correctly, you should take proper care of your collection in order to keep items in the same condition they were at the time you obtained them. The following is a list of things you must never do to your autographs.

• Never glue, staple, or otherwise permanently adhere your autograph to any other material.

• Never put tape on an autograph, even if it is torn. The tape will yellow and crack in time, and your autograph will look worse.

• Never cut or trim a signature or photograph to make it look better. This reduces the value considerably.

• Never cut a signature from a letter. Signed letters are always worth more than simple signatures.

• Never laminate your autograph or enclose it in something that will stick to it. This will completely destroy your autograph.

It is possible to have your autographs repaired, but never attempt to do this on your own, unless you are a specialist in the repair of old papers or documents. There are firms specializing in autograph repair that can do excellent work on your material. One is B&B Gimelson, Inc., 96 S. Limekiln Pike, Chalfont, PA 18914. This firm provides free estimates, and the owner is a collector of autographs.

Framing and matting your autographs can add beauty and value to your signed letters and photographs. This can also add great value to simple signatures if the signatures are framed with photographs or engravings of the subject. Many old engravings of eighteenth and nineteenth century personalities can be found at antiques sales or flea markets, or are available from autograph dealers (the signatures on them are always printed facsimiles). Photographs of virtually any subject can be bought from a number of different sources. It is always wise to frame letters or signatures with engravings or photographs to add attractiveness and interest to the piece.

Sophia Loren, **$20.**

Heather Thomas, **$15.**

It is important to do a professional job when framing or matting material, especially if you plan to sell the item at a later date. No one wants to buy something that is haphazardly constructed, and you certainly wouldn't want to hang the item in your home if it were poorly handled. To do a proper job yourself, you must be careful to select a frame that is of high quality and in an appropriate color. For example, you wouldn't frame an important document signed by George Washington in fluorescent orange. Similarly, a signed pinup photograph of Marilyn Monroe doesn't look right in an antique frame. The choice of the mat is also important as far as color is concerned.

Although it is often very expensive to have a professional frame shop do the work on your autographs, this may be preferable to doing it yourself if you do not know how to mat and frame. Make sure that the frame you select is large enough to hold your unfolded

Lana Turner, **$15.**

letter or signature (even if you want only part of the letter or signature to show through the mat). Also, allow plenty of room for the photograph inside the frame as well. Cutting the mat is the tricky part. You might want to have this done by a professional, or at least check out a book from the library (there are several) that fully explains the technique. The next step is to make two separate openings in the mat, one for the photograph or illustration, and the other for the signature or letter. If you are framing just a signed photograph, there are ready-made mats available at frame shops, and these might be appropriate for you. Carefully measure the size and position on the mat where the items will show through. Mark this off in pencil on the back of the mat. Make your cut with a sharp X-Acto™ knife or razor blade. When assembling the display, be sure that the photograph or other item is backed by acid-free cardboard so it cannot shift.

Whether you choose a professional framer, or elect to do the job yourself, make sure that the matting and backing materials used are guaranteed acid-free. Such materials may be more costly initially, but the added expense is well worth it. Carelessly chosen, acid-containing paper products can actually destroy the investment you are trying to protect. Consult knowledgeable personnel at a good frame shop or art store for guidance in this area.

To preserve your collection, it is not only important to protect it from atmospheric damage, but to also prevent possible financial loss. Therefore, it is a good idea to make a record of your collection for insurance purposes. This might seem tedious and boring, but these records are vital in case of loss, and they create a helpful gauge to measure the strength of your collection.

If you own hundreds of autographs and they are destroyed by fire, you're not going to remember all of them when the time comes for the insurance settlement. Even if you do remember them, you're not going to have exact descriptions and other information (including proof of value) ready to present to your insurance carrier. However, your claim should be processed without problems if you have a box of file cards describing all of the items in your collection. This box of file cards can also serve other purposes for you. You might record the name of the dealer who sold you each item. This might prove useful should you discover later that the items purchased were not authentic. A running inventory of signatures and photographs already in your collection could be maintained so you do not purchase or write for them again (duplication can be a problem with a very large collection). And, if you obtained the items through the mail, you might want to keep a record of the address used next to a description of the autograph in case you wanted to write to the person again or share the address with another collector.

To make the record of your collection, get a packet of file cards and a metal file box. It's an even better idea to make two sets, keeping one at home and one at work, for example. Fill the cards with the following information: name of the person whose autograph it is; type of item (signature, S.P., etc.,); condition; value; name of the dealer who sold you the autograph or the address you received it from through the mail; and a general description of the item or some notes of interest about it. File the cards in alphabetical order or alphabetize them within specialty sections such as "sports" or "movie stars." The cards should be updated frequently to reflect the changing market value of the autographs. A separate file containing photocopies of the actual items could also be prepared and indexed to the collection of file cards.

Like the other steps necessary to properly preserve your autograph collection, keeping accurate records takes time and effort. The work can be tedious, but the aesthetic and financial rewards more than compensate for the effort of learning these new skills.

10

Selling Your Collection

Your investment in autographed material will be much less risky if you know how to sell your items at any time and for the highest possible price. There are many ways to sell duplicate or unwanted autographs, whether they are simple signatures or important historical documents. Each way takes a different amount of work or preparation on your part and, as with anything, the more thought you put into the selling of your autographs, the more you will receive for them.

If you collect autographs through the mail and wish to obtain more autographs, an easy way to increase your collection is to trade autographs with other collectors. By sending more than one photograph or other item to a personality for signature, you will acquire duplicates for trading. Trading can be a great deal of fun, and many collectors are involved in trading groups and partnerships. If you would like to join such a group, place a small classified ad in one of the autograph publications (the UACC's *Pen & Quill* provides free ads to members in every

issue). State that you would like to trade your autographs and list area or areas of specialty.

If trading does not interest you, you can try selling your material to an autograph dealer, making sure that you offer the dealer only the type of items sold in his catalog. In other words, don't try selling your collection of movie star signatures to a dealer who lists only historical documents or literary material in his catalog. Keep in mind that an autograph dealer will not give you the highest possible price for your material. He or she must make a profit, and, therefore, will offer you wholesale prices. Dealers buy items in bulk only, unless you have very important single items, such as a signature of George Washington or a signed photo of Greta Garbo.

The two advantages of selling to dealers are that it saves you the expense of putting together a catalog and becoming a dealer yourself, and it is not necessary for you to authenticate your autographs. A dealer does not expect you to do this, and his

Original self-portrait sketch of director Alfred Hitchcock signed by him and stars of his films. *Clockwise from upper left:* Bob Cummings, Joseph Cotten, Ingrid Bergman, Ruth Roman, James Stewart, Gregory Peck, Tony Perkins, Maureen O'Hara, Sylvia Sidney, Laraine Day, Janet Leigh, Cary Grant, Grace Kelly, and Margaret Lockwood. **$150.**

decision to purchase your material will be based in part on his opinion of the authenticity of your material.

Although most dealers will only buy material outright, there are some who will sell your material in their catalogs on consignment. This means that they will offer your material for sale in their catalogs and, once the items are sold, they will charge you a 20 to 40 percent commission on the sale. Sometimes it is better to consign your material, since you will realize a higher price. The disadvantage lies in the fact that, if your material is not sold, you won't receive any payment at all.

To initiate a consignment arrangement, first write to the dealer explaining that you wish to sell some autographs and asking the dealer if he or she would like to see your material. Never send unsolicited material to a dealer, and always send your material by certified mail, return receipt requested, so that you have a record of the dealer having received your package. Most dealers will make you an offer upon examining the items you are selling, but it is not a bad idea for you to suggest a possible price — just be willing to negotiate.

Selling your autographs by yourself is not easy. The biggest problem you will face is that of authenticity. If you are an unknown seller, possible customers are going to shy away from buying your autographs until you have established a reputation for selling genuine material. However, if your autographs were purchased from reputable dealers, and are accompanied by a receipt and a description of each item signed by the dealer (ask the dealer for these when purchasing material), you should have no problem with authenticity. Also, you might ask other dealers to authenticate items for

you. Most dealers will help you out if you patronize them once in awhile.

If you have only a few items to sell occasionally, you should be able to find a few possible buyers for material that is reasonably priced. Simply place a classified or a display ad in one of the autograph publications. Either list the specific items you are selling, or suggest interested parties contact you for a list of the sale items. Before selling anything, it is wise to do some research regarding the authenticity of your material. You are competing with many other sellers, and collectors are usually careful when buying autographs. Furthermore, selling unauthentic autographs, aside from being unethical, is directly opposed to your best interests as a dealer. This news will travel very quickly in autograph circles and soon put you out of business. It is very important to be an ethical autograph seller, and your honesty will pay off in the long run. Should you accidentally sell some bad material and discover your mistake before the customer does, we strongly advise that you contact the customer immediately and offer a refund.

Individual sales of your duplicate material to other dealers and collectors is one excellent way to refine your collection and finance new acquisitions. However, your very high quality material can be sold at auction, where you could realize close to the full value of your material. There are several auction houses that will handle your material on a commission basis, and there is also the UACC auction, mentioned in chapter 2, that will pay you 75 percent of the sale price. You will not be able to sell insignificant items at auction, however. Auctions are generally reserved for the very interesting

Voice specialist Mel Blanc sends these photographs to all who ask politely. (© 1978 Hanna Barbera Productions, Inc.; © Warner Brothers Inc., 1978.)

and high quality autographs. Nevertheless, they are one of the best ways to sell your choice material short of becoming an autograph dealer, which takes considerably more time and effort.

If you decide to make the leap from collector to collector/dealer, be prepared to spend some time becoming established. Your reputation will grow during this period in direct relationship to how well you have done your homework and the manner in which you have dealt with your clients. You must be skilled in the art of authenticating the autographs you plan to feature in your catalog. Remember, you will be buying inventory as well as selling, and quality control is imperative. Knowledge of current price trends will enable you to buy and sell fairly.

Finding potential customers is not difficult. The UACC publishes an annual mailing list of all its members, and new members' addresses are published in each issue of *The Pen & Quill.* Mailing lists are also available listing subscribers who have expressed an interest in receiving catalogs. Be sure to note your area of specialty in any ads you place. It will save both you and the potential customer time, money, and postage. It is not a good idea to charge for your catalogs at first. Some established dealers do charge for their listings, but, when you are just starting out, you want as many people as possible to read your catalog, and charging for it is not recommended.

Your catalog, or list of autographs for sale, does not have to be fancy, but, if it is well-produced and attractive, customers are more likely to be impressed by your abilities and may patronize you for this reason. At the very least, your catalog should have clean and clear copy. Lists should be typed so that they are easy to read, and they should be printed, not photocopied or mimeographed. After you become more established as a dealer, you may wish to consider having your lists typeset, printed on colored paper with colored ink, or illustrated. Your catalog should explain all abbreviations used and spell out clearly your terms of sale. It should include a money-back guarantee of authenticity,

Rare signed photograph of the original *Our Gang* fat boy, Joe Cobb, **$25.**

Signed photograph of early rock and roll star Bo Diddley. **$20.**

and a return privilege of around five days. You should require payment in advance of shipment for new customers, but be prepared to send out items on approval to customers with established credit. Feature your telephone number in a prominent place, as most customers order by phone. We suggest that you consult a postal chart to determine mail deliveries in various areas. In that way you can stagger the mailings so that all customers will receive the catalog on the same day, and have an equal purchasing opportunity. If customers feel that they aren't being treated fairly, they will stop patronizing you.

As a novice dealer, you must offer reasonable prices. People are hesitant to purchase from a new dealer, unless there is some price attraction. If you scale prices at a lower level, you can increase them gradually, once you have a solid base of frequent customers. Keep in mind that unless you deal in rare and high quality items, such as expensive historical material, you will probably not be able to generate a primary income as an autograph dealer. If you are competent, though, you can build a profitable part-time business and, at the same time, increase your personal collection. Most dealers see a great deal of material and have the first opportunity to purchase the items for themselves at wholesale prices. With time and patience you, too, can become a reputable autograph dealer, make money, build your collection, and still enjoy the hobby.

Many people collect autographs just for the fun of it. But, if your approach to collecting is from the investment standpoint, learning how to sell your autographs is a must. And selling your autographs for the highest possible price will not be as difficult for you if you seek all possible opportunities, are receptive to new information, and are honest in all of your transactions.

Appendix A

Address Sources

A.C.S.
1765 N. Highland Avenue #434
Hollywood, CA 90028
Addresses of personalities in all fields, but specializing in movies, sports, and music. A current list costs $2. Individual addresses sell for $.50 each.

Waterfall Enterprises
1111 Clairmont J-1
Decatur, GA 30030
Address lists of personalities in many fields. Send self-addressed, stamped envelope with your request for more information.

Jim Weaver
405 Dunbar Drive
Pittsburgh, PA 15235
Address lists of personalities in many fields, and lists of celebrities who send free, signed photographs. Send self-addressed stamped envelope with your request for more information.

Auction Houses

Daniel F. Kelleher, Inc.
40 Broad Street
Boston, MA 02109
(617) 523-3676

R.M. Smythe and Co.
24 Broadway
New York, NY 10004
(212) 943-1880

Sotheby's Manuscript Department
34-35 New Bond Street
London W1A2A, England

Autograph Organizations

The Manuscript Society
David R. Smith, Executive Director
350 North Niagara Street
Burbank, CA 91505
Issues a quarterly journal, *Manuscripts*. Annual membership fee is $20.

Universal Autograph Collector's Club
P.O. Box 467
Rockville Centre, NY 11571
Issues a bi-monthly publication, *The Pen & Quill,* featuring addresses and articles on collecting. Sponsors autograph shows, and an annual auction. Annual membership fee is $15.

Autograph Publications

The Autograph Dealer's Directory
Georgia Terry
840 NE Cochran Avenue
Gresham, OR 97030
Published every two years, this publication lists reputable autograph dealers. Send a self-addressed, stamped envelope with your request for more information.

Autograph Digest
One Governor's Lane
Shelburne, VT 05482
Bi-monthly, $5 per year. Published by the author. Features addresses of personalities in all fields, collecting tips, and classified advertising.

The Autograph Review
Jeffrey Morey
305 Carlton Road
Syracuse, NY 13207
Bi-monthly, $9.95 per year. A sports-oriented publication, including addresses, advertising, and collecting tips.

Newsreel Magazine
One Governor's Lane
Shelburne, VT 05482
Bi-monthly, $15 per year. Published by the author. Film-oriented autograph publication featuring addresses, articles, and interviews.

Scene
Published by Waterfall Enterprises (see Address Sources). Publishes addresses and collecting tips. Send self-addressed, stamped envelope for more information.

Books

Axelrod, Todd M., *Collecting Historical Documents — A Guide to Owning History.* Important book with framing, matting, and investment tips. Send a self-addressed, stamped envelope to the American Museum of Historical Documents, 520 South 4th Street, Suite 340, Las Vegas, NV 89109, for more information.

Christensen, Roger and Karen, *The Ultimate Movie, TV, and Rock Directory.* The major source of addresses and facsimiles for popular personalities. Send a self-addressed, stamped envelope to 6065 Mission Gorge Road, San Diego, CA 92120, for more information.

Hamilton, Charles, *Scribblers and Scoundrels* (1968), *Great Forgers and Famous Fakes* (1980), *The Signature of America* (1979), and *American Autographs* (1983). Most of Hamilton's book are out-of-print, but copies are available in larger libraries. They are outstanding sources of autograph facsimiles and other information.

Levine, Michael, *The Address Book: How to Reach Anyone Who's Anyone* (1984). Personality addresses from all fields. Send a self-addressed, stamped envelope to Ampersand, P.O. Box 727, Hollywood, CA 90028 for more information.

Marans, M. Wesley, *Sincerely Yours* (1983). Beautiful book containing the world's best collection of signed photographs. Send a self-addressed, stamped envelope to R.M. Bradley and Co., 250 Boylston Street, Boston, MA 02116 for more information.

Slide, Anthony, *A Collector's Guide to Movie Memorabilia* (1983). Excellent guide to film collecting containing a chapter on autographs.

Smalling, R.J., and Eckes, Dennis W., *The Baseball Address List,* Den's Collector's Den. The source of baseball addresses for virtually every living player. Available in bookstores. Updates are published in *The Autograph Review.*

Photograph Sources

Associated Press
50 Rockefeller Plaza
New York, NY 10020.
Source for photographs of newsmaking personalities of the present and recent past. Send a self-addressed, stamped envelope for more information.

Bureau of Engraving and Printing
U.S. Government, Office
Services Branch
Washington, DC 20228
Photographs and engravings of national leaders and government buildings are available for sale. Send for a price list/order form.

Movie Star News
134 W. 18th Street
New York, NY 10011
The ultimate source of movie star photographs. Send $1 for an illustrated brochure.

NASA
Lyndon B. Johnson Space Center
Houston, TX 77058
Free color photographs of astronauts.

Stephen Sally
Times Square Station
P.O. Box 646
New York, NY 10036
One of the largest collections of inexpensive movie photographs. Send $1 for catalog.

Sy Sussman
2962 S. Mann Street
Las Vegas, NV 89102
Inexpensive photographic source of personalities in many fields. Free catalogs. Send a legal-sized, self-addressed, stamped envelope.

T.C.M.A., Ltd.
P.O. Box 2
Amawalk, NY 10501
Excellent source of sports photographs and other memorabilia. Send a legal-sized, self-addressed, stamped envelope.

Appendix B

Autograph Dealers

Autograph Alcove
6907 W. North Ave.
Wauwatosa, WI 53213
All fields. Free catalogs.

Conway Barker
4126 Meadowdale Lane
P.O. Box 670625
Dallas, TX 75367
All fields. Free catalogs.

Catherine Barnes
2031 Walnut Street Third Floor
Philadelphia, PA 19103
Historical autographs. Free catalogs.

Robert F. Batchelder
1 West Butler Avenue
Ambler, PA 19002
All fields.

Walter R. Benjamin Autographs
P.O. Box 255
Scribner Hollow Road
Hunter, NY 12442
Historical autographs.

Bob Bennett Autographs
One Governor's Lane
Shelburne, VT 05482
Movie autographs and cartoon art.
Free catalogs.

Herman M. Darvick Autographs
P.O. Box 467
Rockville Centre, NY 11571
All fields. Free catalogs.

Fricelli Associates
P.O. Box 247
Bath Beach Station
Brooklyn, NY 11214
All fields. Free catalogs.

Jack B. Good Autographs
P.O. Box 4462
Fort Lauderdale, FL 33338
Movie autographs. Free catalogs.

Paul Hartunian Autographs
65 Christopher Street
Montclair, NJ 07042
All fields. Free catalogs.

Jim Hayes, Antiquarian
P.O. Box 12557
James Island, SC 29412
Historical autographs. Free catalogs.

Jeanne Hoyt Autographs
P.O. Box 1517
Rohnert Park, CA 94928
Popular Material. Free catalogs.

JFF Autographs
P.O. Box U
Manhasset, NY 11030
All fields. Free catalogs.

Brian Kathenes Autographs
Lighthouse Point
P.O. Box 8218
Red Bank, NJ 07701
All fields. Free catalogs.

Stephen Koschal Autographs
P.O. Box 201
Verona, NJ 07044
Historical autographs and signed books. Free catalogs.

Neale Lanigan Autographs
8505 Ridgeway Street
Philadelphia, PA 19111
Movie autographs.

La Scala Autographs
P.O. Box 368
Hopewell, NJ 08525
Opera, music, theater, and dance.

Robert LeGresley Autographs
P.O. Box 576
Topeka, KS 66601
Popular material and cartoon art. Free catalogs.

Lone Star Autographs
P.O. Drawer 500
Kaufman, TX 75142
All fields. Free catalogs.

Monetary Investment, Ltd.
P.O. Box 17246
400 W. Silver Spring Drive
Suite 262
Milwaukee, WI 53217
All fields, historical material. Free catalogs.

Monroe Mendoza
102-10 66th Road
Forest Hills, NY 11375
All modern fields. Inexpensive. Free catalogs.

Kenneth W. Rendell, Inc.
154 Wells Avenue
Newton, MA 02159
Historical autographs.

Paul C. Richards Autographs
High Acres
Templeton, MA 01468
All fields.

Star Signs Autographs
645 S. Harrison Street
Denver, CO 80209
Movie autographs. Free catalogs.

Georgia Terry Autographs
840 NE Cochran Ave.
Gresham, OR 97030
Popular autographs. Free catalogs.

Please note that this is not a complete list of all established dealers. It is provided for the collector's convenience and does not constitute a personal endorsement by the author.

Bibliography

Casey, Douglas R. *Crisis Investing.* New York, NY: Simon and Schuster, 1980.

Christensen, Roger and Karen. *The Ultimate Movie, TV, and Rock Directory.* Cardiff-by-the-Sea, CA: Cardiff-by-the-Sea Publishing Co., 1984.

Darvick, Herman M. *Collecting Autographs.* New York, NY: Julian Messner, 1981.

Hamilton, Charles. *Great Forgers and Famous Fakes.* New York, NY: Crown, 1980.

———. *Scribblers and Scoundrels.* New York, NY: P. Eriksson and Co., 1968.

———. *The Signature of America.* New York, NY: Harper and Row, 1979.

Marans, M. Wesley. *Sincerely Yours.* Boston, MA: Little, Brown, and Co., 1983.

Index

About the Author

Bob Bennett has been collecting autographs since he was thirteen, when he and his brother found the addresses of former baseball players Gus Suhr and Bill "Swish" Nicholson in *Baseball Digest* magazine and wrote away for their autographs. Born in Rutland, Vermont, in 1963, and raised in Vermont and New Jersey, he started collecting autographs seriously in the late 1970s when he joined the Universal Autograph Collectors Club. In 1979 he became a dealer, and this led to his becoming the publisher of *Newsreel Magazine,* the leading film-related autograph publication in the hobby, in 1982. He started a second publication, *Autograph Digest,* in 1983.

His articles about autograph collecting have appeared in *Movie Collector's World* and other publications. He is a Contributing Editor of Hollywood Tribute's *Tribute* magazine, writing the column, "Where Are They Today?" about movie stars of the past. He has been active in the Libertarian movement as a lecturer and writer, and his articles on politics have appeared in several journals and in Vermont's largest newspaper, *The Burlington Free Press.*

Bennett attended the University of Vermont in Burlington, where he graduated with a B.A. in political science in 1985. He is now a student at Albany Law School, in Albany, New York.

143

Price Guide

The following is a general price guide for autographs. Remember that prices are also determined by condition and the content of the letter or document. The prices shown are for actual items listed recently in catalogs from some of the hobby's most reputable dealers. This price guide is also useful for the collector in that it contains the most frequently sold names that appear in autograph catalogs. You will be able to tell not only the proper price to pay, but will be able to judge if the material you want is readily available. Besides the autographs listed herein, autographs of hundreds of other lesser-known individuals can be found in a dealer's catalog. They are often more reasonably priced than the autographs of individuals included here.

Key to Abbreviations

A.L.S.	Autographed Letter Signed
L.S.	Letter Signed
T.L.S.	Typed Letter Signed
D.S.	Document Signed
S.P.	Signed Photograph
A.N.S.	Autographed Note Signed
A.D.S.	Autographed Document Signed

U.S. Presidents

Name	Type	Value
John Adams	Important D.S.	$1,200
John Quincy Adams	D.S. as president	500
	Land grant	175
Chester Arthur	Sig.	125
James Buchanan	A.N.S.	235
Jimmy Carter	S.P.	75
	Sig.	50
Grover Cleveland	T.L.S.	260
	Sig.	75
Calvin Coolidge	D.S.	275
	Sig.	200
Dwight Eisenhower	Book signed	750
	S.P.	325
Millard Fillmore	Sig.	125
	A.LS.	500
Gerald Ford	S.P.	100
	Sig.	75
James Garfield	Sig.	110
Ulysses S. Grant	A.L.S.	750
	Sig.	100
Warren Harding	D.S.	250
Benjamin Harrison	A.D.S.	275
William Henry Harrison	A.D.S.	500
Rutherford B. Hayes	Sig.	95
	D.S.	265
Herbert Hoover	T.L.S.	100
Andrew Jackson	D.S.	850
Thomas Jefferson	D.S. (fair condition)	695
	D.S., important	3,750
Andrew Johnson	D.S., as president	650
Lyndon B. Johnson	Color S.P.	175
John F. Kennedy	D.S.	525
	S.P.	825
Abraham Lincoln	A.N.S.	3,000
	D.S. (3 times)	3,750
James Madison	D.S.	325
William McKinley	Sig.	85
James Monroe	D.S.	110
Richard Nixon	S.P.	80
	Book signed	75
	Sig.	50
Franklin Pierce	L.S. as president	495
	Sig.	100

Name	Type	Value
James Polk	Sig.	$ 250
Ronald Reagan	S.P.	125
	Sig.	70
Franklin D. Roosevelt	L.S.	395
	Sig.	350
Theodore Roosevelt	T.L.S.	800
William H. Taft	Routine T.L.S.	125
	Good content T.L.S.	500
Zachary Taylor	D.S.	400
Harry Truman	T.L.S.	250
	S.P.	195
John Tyler	Sig.	250
Martin Van Buren	A.L.S.	700
George Washington	A.D.S.	3,000
	Hist. imp. L.S. (2 sigs.)	29,500
Woodrow Wilson	L.S.	400
	Sig.	120

Literary Personalities

Name	Type	Value
William Cullen Bryant	A.L.S.	$125
Samuel Clemens (Mark Twain)	Double sig.	275
James Fenimore Cooper	A.D.S.	195
Charles Dickens	Sig.	300
Theodore Dreiser	Book signed	50
Ralph Waldo Emerson	A.L.S.	450
F. Scott Fitzgerald	Book signed	650
Robert Frost	Book signed	150
Zane Grey	Sig.	40
Ernest Hemingway	Ms.S.	1,800
Julia Ward Howe	A.L.S.	125
Victor Hugo	A.L.S.	175
Aldous Huxley	T.L.S.	195
Washington Irving	A.L.S.	200
William James	A.L.S.	250
James Joyce	A.L.S.	1,500
D.H. Lawrence	A.L.S.	1,150
Sinclair Lewis	T.L.S.	30
H. P. Lovecraft	L.S.	550
H. L. Mencken	L.S.	70
Margaret Mitchell	Signed first edition of *Gone with the Wind*	1,250

Name	Type	Value
George Orwell	L.S.	$ 750
George Sand	A.L.S.	175
Upton Sinclair	T.L.S.	75
George Bernard Shaw	A.D.S.	85
Alfred Lord Tennyson	D.S.	125
H. G. Wells	A.L.S.	250
Walt Whitman	Sig.	300
John Greenleaf Whittier	Sig.	40
Kate Douglas Wiggin	A.N.S.	40
Tennessee Williams	S.P.	100

Famous Americans

Name	Type	Value
P.T. Barnum	Sig.	$ 30
	A.N.S.	225
Clara Barton	T.L.S.	250
P.G.T. Beauregard	A.L.S.	375
Alexander Graham Bell	A.L.S.	1,250
William Jennings Bryan	A.L.S.	100
Andrew Carnegie	A.N.S.	75
William F. Cody (Buffalo Bill)	Sig.	250
Jefferson Davis	A.L.S.	475
Walt Disney	Sig.	125
Frederick Douglass	D.S.	125
Thomas Edison	A.N.S. (pencil)	165
	early A.L.S.	1,000
Albert Einstein	Book signed	650
Pat Garrett	L.S.	200
George Gershwin	Sig.	125
	D.S.	750
Jay Gould	A.L.S.	300
Alexander Hamilton	Sig.	485
W. C. Handy	L.S.	195
Patrick Henry	A.L.S.	300
Oliver Wendell Holmes, Jr.	A.L.S.	850
Harry Houdini	T.L.S.	350
Jesse James	L.S.	5,000
Martin Luther King	T.L.S.	200
Charles Lindbergh	T.L.S.	600
Douglas MacArthur	T.L.S.	150
Malcolm X	Sig.	200
Charles Manson	A.L.S.	175
"Bat" Masterson	L.S.	500
J.P. Morgan	L.S.	350

Name	Type	Value
Grandma Moses	Signed Christmas card	$100
Thomas Nast	D.S.	100
Annie Oakley	S.P.	1,500
William Penn	A.L.S.	4,000
Cole Porter	A.Q.S. (musical)	750
John D. Rockefeller	T.L.S.	50
Norman Rockwell	Book signed	125
Eleanor Roosevelt	T.L.S.	40
Margaret Sanger	T.L.S.	75
George Santayana	A.L.S.	150
Sitting Bull	Sig.	900
John Philip Sousa	Sig.	150
Norman Thomas	S.P.	125
Booker T. Washington	T.N.S.	50
Noah Webster	A.L.S.	450
Wilbur Wright	D.S.	450
Brigham Young	L.S.	450

World History

Name	Type	Value
Enrico Caruso	S.P.	$475
Winston Churchill	S.P.	500
Charles Darwin	L.S.	475
Sigmund Freud	S.P.	1,000
Mahatma Gandhi	L.S.	375
George III (King of England)	D.S.	395
Adolf Hitler	Sig.	200
Isabella I (Queen of Spain)	D.S.	900
James II (King of England)	A.L.S.	875
Carl Jung	A.L.S.	1,000
Peter Kropotkin	A.L.S.	100
	A.Q.S.	200
Franz Liszt	A.L.S.	1,000
Louis XIV (King of France)	Sig.	375
Gustave Mahler	S.P.	2,500
Gugliemo Marconi	A.L.S.	275
John Stuart Mill	A.L.S.	800
Benito Mussolini	D.S.	300
Napoleon	Sig. "Nap"	375
Ignace Paderewski	S.P.	150
Joseph Priestley	A.L.S.	875
Camille Saint-Saëns	A.L.S.	175
Jean Paul Sartre	A.Ms.S.	195
Albert Schweitzer	A.L.S.	375
Arturo Toscanini	S.P.	400

Name	Type	Value
Queen Victoria	Sig.	$120
Kaiser Wilhelm	S.P.	455

Cartoonists

Name	Type	Value
Charles Addams	Signed sketch	$50
Joseph Barbera	T.L.S.	10
Jim Davis	Sketch of Garfield	100
	T.L.S.	35
Walt Disney	Daily panel of newspaper cartoon signed by Floyd Gottfredson	1,500
	Signed First Day Cover	125
Chester Gould	Sketch of Dick Tracy	35
Hank Ketcham	Orig. preliminary strip drawing of Dennis the Menace	45
Thomas Nast	Sig.	30
Garry Trudeau	Signed sketch from Doonesbury	45
Raymond Wendelin	Sketch of Smokey the Bear on First Day Cover	80
Chic Young	Sketch of Dagwood Bumstead	50

Movie Stars

Name	Type	Value
Theda Bara	S.P.	$200
John Barrymore	Sig.	100
Wallace Beery	S.P.	125
Humphrey Bogart	Sig.	175
Marlon Brando	S.P.	50
Charlie Chaplin	Self-caricature signed	350
Montgomery Clift	Sig.	85
Bing Crosby	Sig.	40
James Dean	S.P.	800
Frances Farmer	Sig.	70
W. C. Fields	Self-portrait signed	500
Errol Flynn	S.P.	200
Henry Fonda	Signed contract	85
D. W. Griffith	D.S.	325
Buster Keaton	Sig.	75
Charles Laughton	D.S.	200
Laurel and Hardy	S.P., both sigs.	350

Name	Type	Value
Vivien Leigh	S.P.	$250
Carole Lombard	D.S.	200
Jayne Mansfield	S.P.	150
Marx Brothers	Sigs. of all three together	300
Marilyn Monroe	S.P.	650
Basil Rathbone	S.P.	85
Gloria Swanson	S.P.	25
Spencer Tracy	Sig.	95
Ben Turpin	Sig.	65
John Wayne	S.P.	75
Mae West	S.P.	35

Music

Name	Type	Value
Beatles	S.P. (all four)	$800
David Bowie	S.P.	40
Carpenters	S.P. (both sigs.)	20
Johnny Cash	Sig.	5
Roy Clark	S.P.	10
Daryl Hall and John Oates	Both sigs.	25
Michael Jackson	Color S.P.	80
Mick Jagger and Keith Richards	S.P. (both sigs.)	40
Billy Joel	Sig.	5
John Lennon and Yoko Ono	Self-portraits, signed	225
Barry Manilow	Sig.	5
Dolly Parton	S.P.	10
The Police	All three sigs.	50
Elvis Presley	Postcard photo signed	150
Prince	S.P.	100
Carlos Santana	S.P.	15
Pete Seeger	A.Q.S.	25
Simon and Garfunkel	Both signatures	45
Bruce Springsteen	S.P.	90
The Who	S.P. by four original members	100

Sports

Name	Type	Value
Cap Anson	Baseball, sig.	$225
Max Baer	Boxing, sig.	85
Jim Brown	Football, S.P.	25
Roberto Clemente	Baseball, color S.P.	95
Ty Cobb	Baseball, sig.	50

Name	Type	Value
Jim Corbett	Boxing, sig.	$95
Abner Doubleday	Baseball, sig.	250
Chris Evert	Tennis, S.P.	10
Jimmie Foxx	Baseball, S.P.	100
Lou Gehrig	Baseball, sig.	150
Rogers Hornsby	Baseball, sig.	95
Connie Mack	Baseball, sig.	40
John McEnroe	Tennis, S.P.	25
Jesse Owens	Olympics, S.P.	25
Knute Rockne	Football, sig.	60
Bill Russell	Basketball, sig.	20
Babe Ruth	Baseball, sig.	175
Max Schmeling	Boxing, S.P.	15
Tris Speaker	Baseball, sig.	50
Jim Thorpe	Olympics, S.P.	175
Bill Tilden	Tennis, S.P.	35
Gene Tunney	Boxing, D.S.	65
Honus Wagner	Baseball, sig. (pencil)	55
Cy Young	Baseball, sig.	50

Astronauts

Most signatures of the less famous astronauts range from $3-5 ea. Signed photos are $8-12 ea.

Name	Type	Value
Buzz Aldrin	Sm. S.P.	$12
Neil Armstrong	Sig.	15
Michael Collins	S.P.	25
Gordon Cooper	A.N.S.	55
Virgil Grissom (died in space capsule on launch pad)	L.S.	350
Jim Irwin	A.L.S., good content about space flight	35
Sally Ride	Sig. on First Day Cover	20
Wally Schirra	Sig.	5
Alan Shepard	Sig. and quote about space flight	50
Donald K. Slayton	L.S.	40

Authors

Name	Type	Value
Isaac Asimov	Signed bookplate	$10
Peter Benchley	Sig.	5
William Peter Blatty	Signed copy of *The Exorcist*	25
Ray Bradbury	Sig.	5

Name	Type	Value
Vincent Bugliosi	A.N.S.	$5
James MacGregor Burns	Ms.S.	10
Malcolm Cowley	A.L.S.	10
Roald Dahl	Sig.	5
Will Durant	A.L.S.	20
Alex Haley	Ms.S., from "Roots"	45
Joseph Heller	A.L.S.	10
Erica Jong	A.L.S.	20
Stephen King	Sig.	5
Norman Mailer	Limited edition of book signed	75
	Sig.	5
James Michener	Typescript signed	50
Arthur Miller	Sig.	10
Harold Robbins	Sig.	5
Lowell Thomas	Sig.	8
Robert Penn Warren	A.L.S.	20
Thornton Wilder	A.N.S.	50
Herman Wouk	A.Q.S.	40

Criminals

Name	Type	Value
David Berkowitz ("Son of Sam")	Signed quote	$200
Albert DeSalvo (the "Boston Strangler")	L.S.	95
Charles Manson	Sig. on piece of Monopoly money	75
James Earl Ray	A.L.S.	120
Wayne Williams	A.L.S.	80

Military

Name	Type	Value
Sir Douglas Bader	Sig	10
"Pappy" Boyington	Sig.	5
Omar Bradley	Sig.	15
Lloyd Bucher	S.P.	45
Mark Clark	S.P.	15
James Doolittle	S.P.	15
Hyman Rickover	Good content A.N.S.	65
Matthew B. Ridgway	Sig.	8
Paul W. Tibbets	Typescript discussing atomic bomb	100
William C. Westmoreland	Sig.	5

Music and the Arts

Name	Type	Value
George Abbott	A.Q.S.	$35
George Balanchine	Sig.	20
Irving Berlin	D.S., a royalty agreement	375
Leonard Bernstein	Program signed with musical quote	100
	S.P.	30
Eubie Blake	A.L.S.	35
	Sig.	5
Hoagy Carmichael	Sig.	10
Marc Chagall	Signed print	600
Aaron Copland	T.L.S.	12
Salvador Dali	Postcard signed	100
Margot Fonteyn	Program signed	20
Ira Gershwin	Sig.	10
Benny Goodman	Signed First Day Cover	12
Andre Kostelanetz	Sig.	10
Henry Mancini	S.P.	12
Joan Miro	Signed print	100
Eugene Ormandy	T.L.S.	40
Itzhak Perlman	S.P.	30
Artie Shaw	Signed First Day Cover	12
Isaac Stern	D.S.	30
Andy Warhol	Signed print	50
John Williams	Signed First Day Cover	55

Politics

Most signatures of fairly well-known senators, congressmen, and governors (i.e., Howard Baker, Tip O'Neill, or Mario Cuomo) range from $5-$10, with S.P.s at $10-$12. Those of less famous senators, congressmen, and governors range from $2-$3 for signatures, and $5-$10 for S.P.s.

Name	Type	Value
Spiro Agnew	Signed invitation to Nixon inaugural	$80
Carl Albert	T.L.S.	15
Geraldine Ferraro	S.P.	18
John Glenn	Sig.	8
Barry Goldwater	Ms. S.	10
Arthur F. Goldberg	Sig.	10
Hubert Humphrey	Ms.S.	15
Jacqueline Kennedy	S.P.	80

Name	Type	Value
Melvin Laird	S.P.	$8
Henry Cabot Lodge	Ms. S.	10
Thurgood Marshall	Sig.	8
Walter Mondale	Sig.	15
Sandra Day O'Connor	S.P.	8
George Wallace	A.L.S.	20
Earl Warren	L.S.	35

Science, Inventors, and Nobel Prize Winners

Kenneth Arrow	Sig.	$8
Christiaan Barnard	S.P.	15
Milton Friedman	L.S.	15
John Kenneth Galbraith	Sig.	5
Lubos Kohoutek	A.L.S., and S.P.	125
Robert Oppenheimer	L.S.	295
Linus Pauling	Sig.	7
Carl Sagan	Sig.	6
Jonas Salk and Albert Sabin	First Day Cover, both sigs	60
Jonas Salk	Sig.	15
William Shockley	Sig. with sketch of transistor	40
B. F. Skinner	Ms. S.	10
Benjamin Spock	Sig.	15
Edward Teller	S.P.	25
Clyde W. Tombaugh	A.L.S.	100

World Leaders

Yasser Arafat	Signed First Day Cover	$100
Fidel Castro	Sig.	450
King Hussein	S.P.	75
Muammar Khadafy	S.P. with quote	140
Ayatollah Khomeini	Sig.	800
Helmut Kohl	S.P.	10
Anwar Sadat	S.P.	200
Helmut Schmidt	S.P.	15